'A' and 'The' Explained

A LEARNER'S GUIDE TO DEFINITE
AND INDEFINITE ARTICLES

Seonaid Beckwith

Copyright © 2013 by Seonaid Beckwith.

All rights reserved. No part of this publication may be reproduced, distributed or transmitted in any form or by any means, including photocopying, recording, or other electronic or mechanical methods, without the prior written permission of the publisher, except in the case of brief quotations embodied in critical reviews and certain other noncommercial uses permitted by copyright law.

Book Layout ©2013 BookDesignTemplates.com

'A' and 'The' Explained/ Seonaid Beckwith. —1st ed.
ISBN 978-1494245887

Contents

Acknowledgements 8

Section 1: Introduction 10

Section 2: Known And Unknown 12

    Part 2.1: Explanation 12

        2.1.1 Particular and general 12

        2.1.2 Known and unknown 12

    Part 2.2: The listener's surroundings 13

    Part 2.3: Larger situation / general knowledge / unique things 14

    Part 2.4: Information in the rest of the sentence 16

        2.4.1 Relative clauses 16

        2.4.2 Prepositional phrases 17

        2.4.3 *Of*-phrases 18

        2.4.4 Certain adjectives.. 19

        2.4.5 Superlatives 20

    Part 2.5: Something we've already talked about 22

    Part 2.6: We've talked about something connected 25

    Part 2.7: There is / there are 26

    Section 2 Review Exercises 26

Section 3: Specific And General 30

    Part 3.1: Using 'no article' + plural / uncountable nouns to generalise 30

Part 3.2: Difficulties with choosing specific or general 31

    3.2.1 Pre- and post-modification 32

Part 3.3: Using *a/an* + singular countable nouns to generalise 34

Part 3.4: *The* with singular countable nouns to talk about groups of people 35

Part 3.5: *The* with adjectives to talk about groups of people 35

Part 3.6: Using *the* to generalise about nationalities 37

Section 3 Review Exercises 40

Section 4: Using *The* To Talk About Abstract Ideas 43

Part 4.1: *The* with entertainment and recreation 43

Part 4.2: *The* with shops and other businesses 44

Part 4.3: *The* with musical instruments 44

Part 4.4: *The* with transport 45

Part 4.5: *The* with communication and media 47

Part 4.6: *The* with inventions 48

Part 4.7: *The* with parts of the body 48

Part 4.8: *The* with plants and animals 49

Part 4.9: *The* with dances 50

Part 4.10: *The* with geographical expressions 50

Part 4.11: *The* with weather 51

Part 4.12: *The* with certain time words 52

Part 4.13: *The* with grammatical expressions 53

Part 4.14: Other words with *the* 53

Part 4.15: Words which are not like this 54

Section 4 Review Exercises 55

Section 5: Using 'A/An' To Talk About Members Of Categories 62

Part 5.1: Explanation 62

5.1.1 Using one member of a category to generalise 62

5.1.2 Using one member of a category to mean 'it doesn't matter which' 62

Part 5.2: Classifying and describing people or things 64

Part 5.3: Exclamations 67

Section 5 Review Exercises 68

Section 6: Words That Generally Have 'No Article' 71

Part 6.1: Languages, meals and sports 71

6.1.1 Languages 71

6.1.2 Meals 71

6.1.3 Sports 71

6.1.4 Using these words in an unusual way 72

Part 6.2: Time Words 72

6.2.1 Months 73

6.2.2 Days of the week 73

6.2.3 Holidays and special days 73

6.2.4 Dates 73

6.2.5 Parts of the day 74

6.2.6 Seasons 74

6.2.7 Years, decades, centuries and historical periods 74

6.2.8 Using these words in an unusual way 75

Part 6.3: Nouns followed by a classifying letter or number 75

Part 6.4: Newspaper headlines 77

Part 6.5: Unique roles 78

Part 6.6: *Fact is* 79

Section 6 Review Exercises 80

Section 7: Special Cases And Difficulties 82

Part 7.1: Noun adjuncts 82

Part 7.2: Using *a/an* with uncountable nouns 84

Part 7.3: Institutions (*church, university, school* etc.) 87

Part 7.4: *Bed / home / work / town* 89

7.4.1 *Bed* 89

7.4.2 *Home* 90

7.4.3 *Work* (used as a noun) 90

7.4.4 *Town* 91

Part 7.5: Illnesses 91

Part 7.6: Acronyms and initialisms 93

7.6.1 Initialisms 93

    7.6.2 Acronyms 94

Part 7.7: *A little*, and *little*, *a few* and *few* 96

Part 7.8: *Most* and *the most* 98

Part 7.9: *A/an* or *one*? 99

    7.9.1 Choosing *a/an* or *one* 99

    7.9.2 *A/an* and *one* with *half* 101

Part 7.10: Using *a/an* instead of *per* 102

Part 7.11: *Next* and *last* with time expressions 104

Part 7.12: *First / second / third* 106

Part 7.13: *The* with comparatives 107

Section 7 Review Exercises 108

Section 8: Idioms And Fixed Expressions 111

Part 8.1: Prepositional phrases 111

Part 8.2: Idioms 113

Part 8.3: Parallel structures 115

Section 8 Review Exercises 116

Section 9: Proper Nouns 118

Part 9.1: Hints about proper nouns 118

Part 9.2: Geographical names 118

    9.2.1 'No article' 118

    9.2.2 *The* 120

Part 9.3: Places in a city 123

    9.3.1 'No article' 123

    9.3.2 *The* 125

    9.3.3 Either 'no article' or *the* 126

Part 9.4: People's names 128

    9.4.1 'No article' 128

    9.4.2 *The* 128

    9.4.3 *A/an* 129

Section 9 Review Exercises 130

Section 10: Review Exercises 133

Appendix 1: Pronunciation 147

    When to choose *a* or *an* 147

    How to pronounce *the* 148

    Names of letters 148

Appendix 2: Classification Of Nouns 150

    Common and proper nouns 150

    Countable and uncountable nouns 151

        List of common uncountable nouns: 151

        Special cases 154

        Nouns that can be either countable or uncountable 155

    Appendix 2 Review Exercises 157

Appendix 3: *Some* / *Any* / 'No Article' 159

    The difference between *some* and 'no article': 159

    The difference between *some* and *any*: 160

Answers To Exercises 163

    Answers to Section 2 163

    Answers to Section 3 170

    Answers to Section 4 176

    Answers to Section 5 184

    Answers to Section 6 188

    Answers to Section 7 191

    Answers to Section 8 202

    Answers to Section 9 205

    Answers to Section 10 213

    Answers to Appendices 226

Index 233

Acknowledgements

I would like to thank the following people for their enormously helpful comments on earlier drafts: Irina Jonsson, Shehnaz Siddique, Ernest Ćutuk. and especially Jeremy Schaar. Thank you too to all the friends and colleagues who answered my endless questions and to all my students, past and present, whose queries and suggestions have been hugely instrumental in shaping this book.

I also cannot overstate my debt to the many grammarians and academics whose work has influenced my thinking. I would especially like to mention two essential volumes for anyone dealing with this topic: *A Comprehensive Grammar of the English Language* by Quirk, Greenbaum, Leech and Svartvik, and *Practical English Usage* by Michael Swan. I also found the forums at www.wordreference.com extremely interesting and enlightening.

This book would have been much worse without the contribution of Jonathan Wadman, editor extraordinaire, and the sharp eyes and patience of Dorrie Bell. Thanks also go to the talented Jessica Lazare for the cover design.

Finally, thank you to Gill Bell for encouragement and enthusiasm, to David Bell for first showing me that a simple explanation of a difficult concept is both possible and worth striving for, and to William and Elizabeth for inspiration and for putting up with all the time I was working. This book is for Robert, with much love and gratitude.

Section 1: Introduction

Here are a few basic ideas to think about first:

1. We use three articles in English:
    - *a/an* (this is also called 'the indefinite article')
    - *the* (this is also called 'the definite article')
    - 'no article' / 'zero article' (sometimes represented in this book by the symbol Ø).

(We also use *some* and *any*. You can find an explanation of these in Appendix 3.

Of course, we don't write Ø in normal English! I just use it in this book when I want to make it very clear that we need 'no article', not *a/an* or *the*.)

2. We use *a* before a consonant sound and *an* before a vowel sound. See Appendix 1 for more about this.

3. It's very important to understand 'countable' and 'uncountable' nouns when we're talking about articles. A countable noun is often an object. It can make a plural and be counted. For example, *book* is a countable noun. We can say 'one book, two books'. On the other hand, an uncountable noun is often something which isn't one single object. It could be something that's made up of lots of small parts (e.g. *rice*) or it could be an abstract idea (e.g. *love*). Uncountable nouns don't make plurals. For example, we don't usually say 'one rice, two rices'.

For more information about countable and uncountable nouns, including exercises, see Appendix 2.

4. We usually use *a* or *an* before singular countable nouns only:
    - **a** house [singular, countable]
    - **an** orange [singular, countable]

but not

- ~~a houses~~ [plural, countable]
- ~~a luggage~~ [uncountable]
- ~~an information~~ [uncountable].

5. We use 'no article' before plural countable nouns and uncountable nouns only. We usually don't use 'no article' before singular countable nouns:

- I like ∅ cats [plural, countable]
- I like ∅ chocolate [uncountable]

but not

- ~~I like book~~ [singular, countable].

6. We can use *the* before any kind of noun.

7. We don't use articles when there is a possessive pronoun (such as *my*, *his* or *their*), a demonstrative (*this*, *those*), or *each* or *every* in front of a noun.

Section 2: Known And Unknown

Part 2.1: Explanation

2.1.1 Particular and general

Sometimes when we use a noun, we're talking about a specific thing, or a specific set of things. For example, I can talk about one particular book that I have in my mind. I can also talk about a particular set of books. When I do this, I'm not talking about all books. On the other hand, sometimes we want to use a noun in general. I can talk about all the books in the world, about books in general.

In this section, we're going to discuss how to use *a/an* and *the* with a particular noun or a particular group of nouns. We'll discuss how to talk about nouns in general in Section 3.

2.1.2 Known and unknown

When I am thinking of a specific thing or a specific group of things, I use *the* when I think the person listening or reading **will** know (or will be able to work out) which thing or person I'm talking about. On the other hand, I use *a/an* (for singular countable nouns) or 'no article' (for plural and uncountable nouns) when I think the listener or reader **won't** know which thing or person I mean.

The important point is whether the person **who is listening** knows what the speaker is thinking of, or will be able to work it out. We know that the person who is speaking knows which thing(s) he or she means. For example:

- I bought **a** blue sweater yesterday [the speaker knows which sweater, but the listener doesn't, so we use *a*].
- We went to **a** lovely café [the speaker knows which one but the listener doesn't, so we use *a*].

Remember:

- If the listener knows which one(s), we use *the* (with any kind of noun).
- If the listener doesn't know which one(s):

- we use *a/an* with singular countable nouns

- we use 'no article' with plural countable nouns or uncountable nouns.

Sometimes neither the person speaking nor the person listening knows which particular thing or things the speaker is thinking about. We'll discuss this in Section 5. In the rest of this section we'll look at some ways in which the listener might know what the speaker is thinking about.

Part 2.2: The listener's surroundings

Sometimes the listener knows which one we mean because of the place we are in. He or she might be able to see or understand the thing we are talking about. For example:

- Pass me **the** glass [if there's only one glass that we can see, then the listener knows which one I mean, because there's no other choice].
- I'll put **the** dishwasher on [I mean the dishwasher that's in the same room as us].

If there is more than one thing and we are talking about them all, we can still use *the*:

- Please close **the** windows [several windows are open, and I want you to close all of them].

But sometimes, if there is more than one, the listener may not know which one I mean, so I can use *a/an*:

- Please close **the** window [only one is open, so the listener is sure which one I mean].
- Please close **a** window [three are open, so the listener isn't sure which one].

The situation we are in could also be something bigger, like the building, town, city or country we are in. For example:

- I went to **the** cafeteria, but it was closed [the cafeteria in our building].
- You can buy apples at **the** market [the market in our town].

Remember: if we use *the*, it has to be clear to the listener which person or thing we mean.

EXERCISE 2.1

Fill the gap with *a/an* or *the* (this exercise only has singular countable nouns).

1. Sorry, I've spilled water on _____ book [there's only one book on the table so the listener knows which book].

2. Sorry, I've spilled water on _____ book [there are lots of books on the table, and it's not clear to the listener which book].

3. She needs _____ chair from the dining room [the listener can see that there are several chairs in the dining room].

4. She needs _____ chair from the dining room [the listener can see that there's only one chair in the dining room].

5. Would you mind opening _____ door? [I mean the door of the room we are in.]

6. He walked into _____ door and hit his head [the listener doesn't know which door].

7. She fell into _____ river [there's one river in our town].

8. She fell into _____ river [the listener doesn't know which river – it could be any river in the country].

9. I had dinner in _____ Chinese restaurant [I mean the one near our house].

10. I had dinner in _____ Chinese restaurant [there are hundreds in London and the listener doesn't know which one].

Part 2.3: Larger situation / general knowledge / unique things

Above, we saw that we can use *the* when the listener knows which one we mean because of the room or building or town we are in. If there is only one of something in the room, for example, we can use *the* because it's clear which one we mean. For the same reason, we can use *the* with nouns when it's clear to the listener which one we mean because of the country we're in:

- **The** Queen was on television yesterday [if I am in England when I say this, you will understand that I mean the Queen of England].

- I think we should support **the** government [I mean the government of the country that I'm in].

- Our recent problems with **the** economy have really affected **the** middle class [I mean the economy and the middle class of the country that I'm in].

Sometimes, there is only one of something on our planet, or in our solar system, or even in the universe. We use *the* with these words, as it's clear which one we mean. For example, we use *the* with *sun* as there's only one sun close to us and everybody knows which one we mean:

- **The** sun was very hot that day.

In the same way, we often use *the* if there is only one group of something:

- I loved learning about **the** planets in school.

Here is a list of some words (sometimes called 'unique things') that are often used in this way:

the sun	Don't look directly at **the** sun.
the moon	She could see **the** moon from her bedroom window.
the stars	**The** stars are difficult to see clearly.
the sky	**The** sky was a lovely shade of blue.
the universe	**The** universe is vast.
the planets	I would love to visit **the** planets.
the world	It's the best city in **the** world.
the solar system	The alien travelled to the edge of **the** solar system.
the air	The bird flew off into **the** air.

Of course, we can also use many of these words as normal nouns, if we need to. When I say 'the moon', you understand that I mean our moon, the moon that circles the earth. But Jupiter (for example) also has moons. In this case, I can use 'moon' as a normal noun:

- Jupiter has **a** moon called Io.

See also Part 4.15 for words that seem to be unique, but are not used in this way.

Part 2.4: Information in the rest of the sentence

Sometimes the listener knows which one we mean because we make it clear in our sentence, by using certain grammar or vocabulary.

2.4.1 Relative clauses

We can use different grammatical structures to say which one we mean. We often use relative clauses. For example:

- John knows **the** girl that I met yesterday.

Remember, it needs to be clear to the listener which one we mean from the relative clause plus what the listener knows. If it's not obvious, and the listener doesn't know which one we're talking about, we can still use *a/an* even if we use a relative clause.

For example:

- I saw John talking to **a** girl that I met last night. [Even though there is a relative clause, I think the listener may not know exactly which girl, so I use *a*. Maybe I met several girls last night, or maybe the listener wasn't with me last night, so he doesn't know which girl I mean.]

- I saw John talking to **the** girl that I met last night. [I can use *the* because I think the listener does know which girl I mean. Maybe the listener also met the girl last night, for example.]

Even if you give lots of information about the noun, you can still use *a/an* if you think the listener doesn't know which one you mean:

- I met **a** girl last night who has red hair and who was wearing a black dress and whose mother is a doctor.

EXERCISE 2.2

Fill the gap with *the* if the listener knows which one from the rest of the sentence, or use *a/an* if the listener doesn't know (I'm assuming that, for this exercise, the relative clause makes it clear to the listener which one).

1. I drank _____ cup of coffee that I'd just bought.

2. I drank _____ cup of coffee.

3. John's going out with _____ French girl who we met last week.

4. John's going out with _____ French girl.

5. I bought _____ new laptop.

6. I bought _____ laptop that I told you about.

7. David had dinner in _____ restaurant.

8. David had dinner in _____ restaurant that he usually goes to.

9. He played _____ piece of music.

10. He played _____ piece of music that we were discussing yesterday.

2.4.2 Prepositional phrases

In the same way, we often use prepositional phrases (*on the table*, *by the station*, *under the desk*, *in the cupboard*) to say which one we mean. For example:

- Pass me **the** book on the table [we can see that there's only one book on the table, so it's clear which one I mean].

- I often go to **the** café by the station [the listener lives in my town, so I think he knows about that particular café].

- Could you grab **the** brush in the cupboard? [I know there's only one brush, so when you open the cupboard, you will see which brush I mean.]

As with relative clauses, we only use *the* with a prepositional phrase if we think the listener will know which one we mean or will be able to work out which one we mean. For example:

- I've left **a** book on the table [maybe the listener didn't see which book].

- I often go to **a** café by the station [maybe the listener doesn't know my town, so he doesn't know which café I mean].

EXERCISE 2.3

Fill the gap with *the* if the listener knows which one from the rest of the sentence, or use *a/an* if the listener doesn't know (I'm assuming that, for this exercise, the prepositional phrase makes it clear to the listener which one).

1. Let's meet in _____ café.

2. Let's meet in _____ café next to my flat.

3. I picked up _____ piece of paper on the floor.

4. I picked up _____ piece of paper.

5. Could you put these flowers on _____ table?

6. Could you put these flowers on _____ table next to the door?

7. I put my new cushion on _____ chair.

8. I put my new cushion on _____ chair next to the fireplace.

9. She bought a new dress in _____ shop.

10. She bought a new dress in _____ shop next to the supermarket.

2.4.3 *Of*-phrases

We often use *of*-phrases, such as *the back of,* to tell the listener which one we mean. Because something only has one back, for example, we usually use *the* when we talk about it, as we expect the listener to be able to work out which back we mean. Here is a list of some words that we can use in this way:

the back of	I wrote her number on **the** back of my notebook.
the front of	**The** front of the dress was blue.
the middle of	She sat down in **the** middle of the floor.
the top of	He stood at **the** top of the stairs and waited.
the bottom of	The answers are at **the** bottom of the page.
the edge of	I tripped on **the** edge of the pavement.
the beginning of	At **the** beginning of the book, she is living in Paris.
the end of	They got married at **the** end of the film.
the height of	What's **the** height of Mount Fuji?
the length of	He ran **the** length of the football pitch.
the size of	I was amazed at **the** size of his house.
the weight of	I can't guess **the** weight of the cake.
the title of	What's **the** title of the film that we saw last week?
the price of	**The** price of flats here is very high.

2.4.4 Certain adjectives

In the same way, there are some adjectives which we often use to talk about only one thing (or one group of things). For example, if I say 'the last bus' I use *the* because only one bus can be last, so the listener knows which one I mean. Here's a list of adjectives that we often use with *the* when they are followed by nouns:

same	He was wearing **the** same T-shirt as me.
next	Let's get on **the** next train that comes.
last	We caught **the** last bus home.
only	Coffee is **the** only thing I want right now.
right / correct	It's **the** right answer.
wrong*	I'm afraid that's **the** wrong answer.
usual	We went to **the** usual restaurant.

*It is a bit strange to talk about 'the wrong answer' when there are usually lots of wrong answers to any question, but it is correct.

See Part 7.11 for *next* and *last* with time expressions. See also Part 7.12 for a similar use of *first/second/third*.

EXERCISE 2.4

Fill the gap with *a/an* or *the*.

1. Julie crashed her bike into _____ tree.

2. Julie crashed her bike into _____ only tree in her garden.

3. We went to _____ restaurant.

4. We went to _____ usual restaurant.

5. John has _____ yellow car.

6. John has _____ same yellow car as Mike.

7. Let's get _____ taxi.

8. Let's get _____ next taxi.

9. He brought _____ cake.

10. He brought _____ wrong cake.

11. She put down _____ card and won the game.

12. She put down _____ right card and won the game.

2.4.5 Superlatives

If we use a superlative adjective ('**the tallest** student in the class') then there is obviously only one (or one group) of the thing we are talking about. There is one student who is the tallest in the class, and because it's clear to the listener which one we mean, we usually use *the*:

- She's **the** most beautiful girl I've ever seen.
- It's **the** best café in London.
- John and Lisa are **the** most intelligent students here.
- This bowl is **the** biggest one.

Remember, we don't use *the* when there is a possessive:

- He's my best student.
- That's our most important goal.

It's possible to drop *the* when the adjective is used later in the sentence, rather than directly before the noun. We can choose either *the* or 'no article', with no change in meaning:

- She is (the) most beautiful.
- This café is (the) best.
- John and Lisa are (the) most intelligent.
- This bowl is (the) biggest.

This is not possible when the adjective comes directly before the noun:

- ~~He is fastest swimmer~~.

EXERCISE 2.5

Fill the gap with *the* if it's necessary. If you can choose, use 'no article' (Ø).

1. Everest is _____ highest mountain in the world.

2. Who is _____ oldest person in your family?

3. This dress was _____ cheapest.

4. Which language do you think is _____ easiest to learn?

5. This book is _____ most serious one on the topic.

6. I think that one over there is _____ strongest horse.

7. This film is _____ shortest.

8. She's _____ fastest runner in her school.

9. That suitcase is _____ lightest.

10. Out of all the cities in Europe, London is _____ biggest.

With superlative adverbs, we can also choose to use *the* or 'no article':

- Luke reads (the) fastest.
- I like vanilla ice cream (the) best.
- She can speak six languages, but she speaks Spanish (the) most confidently.

These examples all compare one person or thing with other people or things. However, sometimes we compare a person or thing in one situation with the same person or thing in a different situation. In this case, when the superlative adjective or adverb is later in the sentence, we usually don't use *the*.

Compare these two sentences:

- I'm Ø most productive early in the morning [I'm more productive in the morning than I am in the afternoon or the evening].
- I'm **the** most productive early in the morning [I'm more productive than the other people in my office first thing in the morning].

More examples:

- Julie does swimming, running and cycling. She's always Ø most tired after cycling.

- John types Ø most quickly when he's drunk a lot of coffee!

- Tea is Ø best when you drink it very hot.

- London is Ø most depressing in January.

EXERCISE 2.6

If it's possible to choose between *the* and 'no article', put *the*. Otherwise, put 'no article' (Ø).

1. I read a lot of books on the subject and this one is _____ best.

2. I wake up _____ earliest on Mondays, as I go to a yoga class. On other days I sleep later.

3. Amanda's _____ happiest when she's on holiday.

4. Which student in the class is _____ happiest?

5. This juice is _____ most delicious if you chill it for a long time first.

6. The British Library is _____ best in the mornings. It's too crowded in the afternoons.

7. John is _____ calmest when he's working.

8. Of all the people in our office, Adrian is _____ calmest.

9. Lucy wakes up _____ earliest in her family.

10. Which juice is _____ most delicious? Apple juice, orange juice or raspberry juice?

See also Part 7.8 for *most* and *the most*.

Part 2.5: Something we've already talked about

The listener might know which one we mean because we've already talked about the thing in our conversation (or piece of writing):

- I bought **an** apple and an orange. **The** apple was delicious.

I use *an* at first because I think the person listening won't know which apple or which orange I am talking about. But the second (or third or fourth...) time I talk about something, I can use *the* because the listener knows which one. He or she knows because I've already said which one – it's the apple that I bought yesterday (for example) and not another apple.

However, notice that this use of *the* is not very common, because usually when we talk about a thing or person more than once, we use a pronoun the second (or third or fourth...) time:

- I bought **an** apple. **It** was delicious. **It** was very juicy and **it** had shiny red skin.

EXERCISE 2.7

Fill the gaps with *a* or *the*.

1. He gave me _____ clock and _____ picture as a wedding present. _____ clock belonged to his grandmother.

2. I took _____ suitcase and _____ backpack on holiday. _____ suitcase was much more useful.

3. John broke _____ vase when he was in Marie's house. _____ vase was over 100 years old.

4. Julie read _____ book and _____ magazine. She said _____ book was quite boring, though.

5. I washed _____ white shirt and _____ red top together. Now _____ shirt is pink.

Again, we can't use *a/an* with uncountable nouns or plural countable nouns. In these cases, if we are introducing something for the first time that our listener doesn't know about, we use 'no article', not *a/an*. (We can also use *some* or another word that tells us the amount depending on the situation: see Appendix 3.)

- I bought beef, vegetables and milk. **The** beef was very good.

- Her house is full of DVDs and books. **The** books are mostly about Africa.

EXERCISE 2.8

Fill the gaps with *a/an* or 'no article' (Ø). (Remember, all of these are being introduced for the first time and we think the listener doesn't know which one(s) we mean.)

1. She gave us _____ bread and _____ orange juice. The orange juice was delicious.

2. I got _____ book and _____ magazine from the library.

3. We watched _____ films and _____ TV programmes all night. The films were better.

4. She offered us _____ piece of cake or _____ biscuits.

5. We had _____ broccoli and _____ cheese for dinner.

6. I dropped _____ glass and two bowls. They all broke.

7. We cooked _____ spaghetti and _____ bacon. John had bought the spaghetti in Rome.

8. She has _____ black umbrella and I have _____ blue one. The blue one is much bigger.

9. We had _____ piece of pie and _____ potatoes for lunch. The pie was very good indeed.

10. I took _____ bottle of wine and _____ box of chocolates to the party.

11. I drank _____ cup of coffee and ate _____ biscuits. The biscuits had been made by my mother.

12. She bought _____ shoes and _____ dress to wear to her sister's wedding.

13. Ruth has _____ son and _____ two daughters. One of the daughters is in my class.

14. They drank _____ water and _____ tea.

15. At the weekend, I crashed my bike into _____ car.

16. I moved into _____ new flat last month. It's really lovely.

17. Could you get _____ milk and _____ bar of chocolate when you are at the shop?

18. I had _____ pasta and _____ glass of wine last night. The pasta was really good.

19. I spilled _____ coffee on the sofa and I dropped _____ jug of milk on the floor.

20. John has _____ orange chairs and _____ green carpets!

We can also use *the* after we have introduced something and then we use a different word to talk about the same thing:

- A female student came in. **The** girl … [Here, *the girl* is the same person as *a female student* so the listener knows which one we mean because we have already mentioned her.]

Again, we often use a pronoun, rather than *the + noun* in this case:

- A female student came in. **She** …

Part 2.6: We've talked about something connected

We can also use *the* to talk about things which we haven't already talked about directly but which we can understand from something else that we've said. In the example below, we know that houses have front doors:

- We arrived at a house. **The** front door was open. [In this case we know *the front door* is the door of the house we've just talked about. We think the listener will understand which door we mean, but we use *a* when we introduce the house because we don't think the listener will know which house we mean.]

- I wanted to buy a new coat but **the** sleeves were too long. [We think our listener will understand that we mean 'the sleeves of the coat that I just mentioned'.]

- We went for a walk in the park. **The** lake was frozen and **the** ducks looked cold. [We think our listener will understand that we mean 'the lake and the ducks in the park that I just mentioned'. Even though not all parks have lakes or ducks, it's quite common.]

- I've just joined a new gym. **The** swimming pool is very big. [We think our listener will understand that we mean 'the swimming pool in the gym that I just mentioned'. Again, not all gyms have swimming pools, but many do.]

On the other hand, if the second noun is something that isn't always (or isn't often) connected with the first noun, then we use *a/an* or 'no article' in the usual way. In the example below, we know that houses don't usually have lorries outside:

- We arrived at a house. **A** lorry was parked outside.

EXERCISE 2.9

Fill the gaps with *a/an* or *the*.

1. I bought _____ new dress, but I was annoyed to find that _____ zip was broken.

2. They stopped for _____ picnic. However, _____ lemonade was warm.

3. Amelia went to _____ restaurant. She saw _____ famous actress there.

4. She sat down on _____ chair, and started reading _____ book.

5. They hired _____ car on holiday, but when they opened _____ boot, _____ cat was hiding inside!

Part 2.7: There is / there are

On the other hand, we use some expressions when we **don't** think that the listener will know which thing(s) we mean. One of these expressions is *there is / there are*.

There in English has two meanings. The first meaning is 'in a certain place'. For example:

- Your keys are **there** [*there* = 'on the table'].

- **There** are the books that I lost! [*There* = 'under the bed'].

When *there* means 'in a certain place', there is no special article use. In 'there are the books that I lost' I use *the* because I explain which books I mean with the relative clause 'that I lost' (see Part 2.4.1). We often stress *there* when it has this meaning.

The second use of *there* means 'something exists'. For example:

- **There's** a post office in my town. ['A post office exists in my town' – I don't say exactly where it is.]

- **Is there** a bank nearby? ['Does a bank exist nearby?']

- **There are** two train stations in Glasgow. ['Two train stations exist in Glasgow.']

- **There are** butterflies in my garden. ['Butterflies exist in my garden.']

- **There is** always traffic on this road. ['Traffic always exists on this road.']

In this second case, we very often use *a/an* with a singular noun. With a plural noun, it's normal to use a number, or 'no article'.

Section 2 Review Exercises

EXERCISE 2.10

Choose *a/an*, *the* or 'no article' (Ø).

1. William is _____ cutest baby in London.

2. Let's start again from _____ beginning of the song.

3. I bought _____ new dress.

4. Which is your favourite city in _____ world?

5. He was wearing _____ same T-shirt as his brother.

6. I'll meet you in _____ usual place.

7. This is _____ only dress I could find.

8. Today is _____ coldest day of the year.

9. I bought _____ wrong book.

10. He bought a pen and some paper in the shop. _____ pen was red.

11. She crashed her bicycle into a car and broke _____ wheel.

12. She lay on her back on the grass and looked at _____ sky.

13. Everest is _____ highest mountain in the world.

14. I had _____ cup of tea and _____ biscuit. They were both delicious.

15. Please pass _____ water jug [there is one water jug on our table].

16. Have you read _____ book that I lent you?

17. I love looking at _____ planets on a clear night.

18. There's _____ dirt all over his jeans.

19. What's _____ title of the film that you saw last night?

20. There's _____ post office near the bank.

EXERCISE 2.11

Choose *a/an*, *the* or 'no article' (Ø).

1. The page number is at _____ bottom of each page.

2. How many planets are in _____ solar system?

3. We ate _____ sandwiches and drank _____ water.

4. I bought a new dress. It has a pattern on _____ sleeves.

5. I had _____ cup of coffee for breakfast.

6. I met a man and a woman last night. _____ woman was from Mexico.

7. She bought _____ new laptop.

8. There are _____ people outside.

9. She wants to sit in _____ armchair [there is only one armchair in this room].

10. In the countryside, you can see _____ stars much more clearly than in the city.

11. There's _____ good hairdresser on that road.

12. I had _____ bread and cheese for lunch.

13. It's not good for your eyes to look directly at _____ sun.

14. Where's _____ shop that John works in?

15. I've got _____ tent, but it's very old. You can borrow it if you want.

16. They went for a walk and looked at _____ moon.

17. It's on _____ back of the page.

18. She gave me _____ last chocolate.

19. She put _____ book in her bag [you don't know which book].

20. She bought _____ laptop that her brother recommended.

EXERCISE 2.12

Choose *a/an*, *the* or 'no article' (Ø).

1. I had lunch in a lovely restaurant. _____ main course was excellent.

2. Julie has _____ sister and two brothers.

3. Please pass me _____ coffee on the table [there is one cup of coffee and one table near us].

4. Sorry, that's _____ wrong book. I need the one by David Jones.

5. It's amazing to think about how big _____ universe is.

6. John is _____ tallest in his family.

7. There are _____ spiders in the bath.

8. We rented _____ car on holiday.

9. She walked into a beautiful house. _____ kitchen was near _____ front door.

10. There's _____ Japanese restaurant near my house.

11. The artist's name is on _____ back of the painting.

12. I bought _____ new computer.

13. My brother is in _____ middle of the photo.

14. She got _____ new shoes last weekend.

15. Which is _____ right answer?

16. There's _____ luggage in the hall.

17. This is _____ most beautiful painting that I've ever seen.

18. I visited _____ old castle yesterday.

19. I bought a new bicycle, but _____ seat is really uncomfortable.

20. At _____ end of the book, they fell in love.

(Remember that you can download all the exercises as printable PDFs at www.perfect-english-grammar.com/a-and-the.html.)

Section 3: Specific And General

Part 3.1: Using 'no article' + plural / uncountable nouns to generalise

As we saw in Section 2, sometimes when we use a noun, we want to talk about a particular thing (or a particular group of things). For example, I might have a certain car in my mind. If I think the person that I'm talking to knows which car I mean, I use *the*, and if I think the person that I'm talking to doesn't know which car I mean, I use *a/an*:

- I've bought **a** new car [I'm thinking of a certain car, but the listener doesn't know which one, so I use *a*].
- I've bought **the** car that we saw last week [I'm thinking of a certain car and the listener does know which one, so I use *the*].

On the other hand, sometimes we want to talk about cars in general. In this case, I'm not thinking of a particular car or group of cars. Instead I'm thinking about all the cars in the world, about the category of cars. I want to say something about cars in general:

- Ø Cars cause a lot of pollution.

Usually, when we are talking in general, we use 'no article' (Ø). Remember, we usually can't use 'no article' with singular countable nouns, so if you want to talk in general with 'no article' you must use either a plural countable noun, or an uncountable noun:

- She loves Ø cat**s** [not 'she loves cat'].
- He hates Ø mushroom**s** [not 'he hates mushroom'].
- Children need Ø love ['love' is uncountable].

This is by far the most common way to talk about something in general in English.

EXERCISE 3.1

Fill the gap with *the* (if we're talking about a particular noun or group of nouns) or 'no article' (Ø) (if we're talking in general).

1. He hates _____ cats.

2. I like _____ cats that you have.

3. I gave her back _____ books that she'd lent me.

4. _____ books are expensive.

5. _____ rice is very popular in Asia.

6. Pass _____ rice please [it's on our table].

7. It's impressive how clever _____ dogs are.

8. _____ dogs that my friend has are really stupid.

9. Many people say _____ love that you feel for your baby is exceptionally strong.

10. _____ love is more important than money.

11. She loves _____ flowers – you could buy her some for her birthday.

12. I put _____ flowers that I received for my birthday in a vase.

13. _____ chocolate is made from cocoa.

14. She put _____ chocolate that she bought in the fridge.

15. I dropped _____ cakes that you made on the way to the party.

16. She likes making _____ cakes.

17. _____ lions in London Zoo are quite friendly.

18. _____ lions are very scary animals.

19. Do you think _____ money is important for a happy life?

20. I need _____ money that I left on the table.

Part 3.2: Difficulties with choosing specific or general

Sometimes the line between specific and general is not clear. For example:

- The books on the table are mine [clearly specific].
- Books are useful [clearly general].

but

- It's important for young people to have access to (the) books in the library [we can choose *the* or 'no article'].
- (The) books in England are quite expensive [we can choose *the* or 'no article'].

There isn't a clear, definite line between general and specific, and in the middle it's often possible to choose either *the* or 'no article'. In situations where we can choose, using *the* makes it clear that we think the listener knows which particular group of things or people we're talking about. I'm afraid that there are no really clear rules about this, but I list some tips below to help you decide if the noun is general or specific below.

3.2.1 Pre- and post-modification

We often use nouns in a general way, even if they have an adjective (or noun adjunct – see Part 7.1) in front. For example, we say:

- I love Ø Italian coffee.

This is talking about Italian coffee in general. If I'm talking about a particular Italian coffee and I think the listener understands which coffee I mean, then of course I can use *the* in the normal way:

- I love **the** Italian coffee that they serve in this café.

In the same way, here are some other nouns which are used in a general way, but have an adjective or noun adjunct in front:

- I love Ø red wine.
- The company imports Ø British beef.
- Ø 1920s music is very popular in London just now.
- He wrote his thesis on Ø 21st-century art.
- I enjoy studying Ø French philosophy.
- She hates Ø vegetable soup.

Sometimes the choice between general and specific depends more on the grammar of the sentence than the meaning of the words. As we saw above, we often use 'no article' when there is an adjective before the noun. However, when we follow the noun with the preposition *of*, we tend to use *the*, even when the meaning is the same:

- **The** music **of** the 1920s is very popular in London just now.

- I enjoy studying **the** philosophy **of** France.

When the noun has a different preposition (not *of*) then it's less likely to need *the*. In this case, it's often possible to choose either *the* or 'no article', with no change in meaning:

- I love (the) coffee **from** Italy.

EXERCISE 3.2

Fill the gap with *the* or 'no article' (Ø).

1. We studied _____ German philosophy.

2. We read about _____ poetry of Scotland.

3. He's interested in _____ human happiness.

4. I took a class on _____ French literature.

5. The book's about _____ music of Ireland.

6. I've never studied _____ art of the Far East.

7. I watched a programme on TV about _____ twentieth-century ideas.

8. She writes about _____ modern art.

9. She's writing her thesis on _____ philosophy of Hegel.

10. I read an article about _____ history of South America.

11. She read a book about _____ philosophy of Kant.

12. He likes _____ eighteenth-century poetry.

13. There was a documentary about _____ literature of the United States.

14. Could you tell me more about _____ Indian music?

15. There was an article in the paper about _____ Italian art.

16. He likes discussing _____ ideas of the Greek philosophers.

17. They studied _____ science of the natural world.

18. We listened to a lecture on _____ work of Leonardo da Vinci.

19. They are very interested in _____ Chinese calligraphy.

20. We read about _____ British history.

Part 3.3: Using *a/an* + singular countable nouns to generalise

It is also possible to use *a* or *an* with a singular countable noun when we want to use one member of a group as an example to say something about the whole group in general. For example:

- **A** male lion has a long mane.
- **An** accountant must be good with numbers.
- **A** child needs love.

These examples are almost the same as using a plural with 'no article'. So, we can also say (and the meaning is really the same):

- Ø Male lions have long manes [= all male lions, male lions in general].
- Ø Accountants must be good with numbers [= all accountants].
- Ø Children need love [= all children].

You can usually choose if you'd like to use 'no article'+ plural noun or *a/an* + singular countable noun. 'No article' + plural or uncountable noun is the most usual way to generalise. *A/an* + singular countable noun often sounds a little more formal.

Notice that we can't use *a/an* + singular countable noun to generalise when we mean all or some of the members of a group, but only when we're using one member of the group as an example. When we say 'a male lion has a long mane', this is true for each male lion. Each lion has his own mane. Equally, each child needs its own love, and each accountant must be good with numbers.

On the other hand, we can't say 'a panda is endangered'. This means only one panda, not all of them. Instead, we can say 'pandas are endangered' (see Part 3.1) or 'the panda is endangered' (see Part 4.8).

EXERCISE 3.3

Fill the gap with *a/an* + singular noun if it's possible. If not, use 'no article' (Ø) + plural noun.

1. It's important for _____ (nurse) to be kind and friendly.

2. _____ (nurse) from all the hospitals in the country went on strike last week.

3. _____ (car) need / needs to be cleaned from time to time.

4. _____ (car) cause / causes huge environmental problems.

5. _____ (plant) have / has roots, stems and leaves.

6. Without _____ (plant), humans couldn't live.

7. _____ (tiger) eat / eats meat.

8. _____ (tiger) kill / kills a few people a year, but most tigers don't attack people.

See also Section 5 for information about using *a/an* with member of categories.

Part 3.4: *The* with singular countable nouns to talk about groups of people

It's possible to use *the* + singular countable noun to talk about a whole category of people. This sounds quite formal. It's as if we are talking about 'the typical example of this group'.

- Banks should pass on savings to **the** customer [= to customers].

- We should consider how these changes to classes will affect **the** student [= will affect students].

- He spoke with the experience of **the** seasoned musician [= with the kind of experience that seasoned musicians usually have].

Part 3.5: *The* with adjectives to talk about groups of people

Usually, of course, we need to have a noun before we can use *a* or *the*. But we can use some adjectives as nouns when we want to talk about the group of people described by the adjective. In this case, we can use *the* + adjective.

For example, *the unemployed* means the same as *unemployed people*. *The unemployed* is more formal, and is much more likely in formal writing, such as newspaper articles. Here are some adjectives that are often used as nouns in this way:

deaf	We should have an interpreter for **the** deaf.
disabled	The government gives a lot of help to **the** disabled.
elderly	**The** elderly are an important voting group.
homeless	**The** charity works with the homeless.
hungry	That charity gives food to help **the** hungry.
old	**The** old are often frightened to go out at night.
poor	**The** poor don't get enough help.
powerful	The weak can be exploited by **the** powerful.
rich	**The** rich often have access to the best schools.
uneducated	This program aims to teach maths to **the** uneducated.
unemployed	This idea helps get **the** unemployed back into work.
weak	Many people believe that it's good to help **the** weak.
young	**The** young are very comfortable using computers.

These adjectives take a plural verb. It's also important to note that sometimes this use might not be very polite. It's often better to say 'deaf people' rather than 'the deaf', for example, as using 'the deaf' focusses only on the person's deafness, rather than talking about a person who happens to be deaf.

EXERCISE 3.4

Fill the gap with *the* or 'no article' (Ø) (all of the sentences are talking about the group in general).

1. _____ young people spend too much time on the internet.

2. _____ young spend too much time on the internet.

3. The government has a duty to protect _____ poor.

4. The government has a duty to protect _____ poor people.

5. How can we find work for all _____ unemployed?

6. How can we find work for all _____ unemployed people?

7. She works with _____ deaf people.

8. She works with _____ deaf.

9. Is it a good idea to raise taxes for _____ rich?

10. Is it a good idea to raise taxes for _____ rich people?

11. I try to help _____ homeless if I can.

12. I try to help _____ homeless people if I can.

13. It's wrong to exploit _____ weak.

14. It's wrong to exploit _____ weak people.

15. _____ elderly are often lonely.

16. _____ elderly people are often lonely.

17. This charity helps _____ hungry all over the world.

18. This charity helps _____ hungry people all over the world.

19. This exclusive restaurant is popular with _____ wealthy people.

20. This exclusive restaurant is popular with _____ wealthy.

Part 3.6: Using *the* to generalise about nationalities

We can also use *the* + adjective with nationality adjectives to generalise about a whole group:

- **The** French usually eat late [this is the same as saying 'French people usually eat late' – you can see it's general reference as it talks about all French people].

- **The** Japanese tend to think education is very important.

However, we can only do this if the nationality adjective has a different form to the noun that means 'a person from that country'. For example, if we are talking about Spain, the adjective is *Spanish* (Spanish people, Spanish food). *Spanish* is not a noun that means 'a person from Spain'. We **can't** say 'I met a Spanish last night'. There is a noun which means a Spanish person: *Spaniard*. In this case, the noun and the adjective have different forms, so when we want to talk about all the people from Spain, we can say 'the Spanish'.

On the other hand, if we want to talk about Canada, the adjective is *Canadian* (Canadian people, Canadian music). But *Canadian* can also be a noun. We **can** say 'I met a Canadian last night'. In this case, the adjective form and the noun form are the same, so we can't use *the Canadian* to talk about all the people from Canada. *The Canadian* means one specific Canadian person. Instead, we can use *Canadians*.

In general, if the adjective ends in *-ish* or *-ese*, we can use it with *the* to talk about the whole group:

- **The** British / British people
- **The** Portuguese / Portuguese people

Also:

- **The** Swiss / Swiss people
- **The** Dutch / Dutch people

On the other hand, if the nationality adjective ends in *-an*, it's often also used as a noun. In this case, we often use 'no article' + plural noun to generalise, in the normal way:

- Ø Algerians
- Ø Americans
- Ø Australians
- Ø Austrians
- Ø Colombians
- Ø Croatians
- Ø Germans
- Ø Indonesians
- Ø Lithuanians
- Ø Moroccans
- Ø Russians

Other examples (that don't end in *-an*) include:

- Ø Czechs
- Ø Pakistanis
- Ø Thais

EXERCISE 3.5

Fill the gap with 'no article' + plural noun if it's possible. If it's not possible, use *the* + adjective.

1. _____ (Scottish) like chocolate.

2. _____ (Kenyan) like chocolate.

3. _____ (Brazilian) like chocolate.

4. _____ (Chinese) like chocolate.

5. _____ (Swedish) like chocolate.

6. _____ (Italian) like chocolate.

7. _____ (Turkish) like chocolate.

8. _____ (Polish) like chocolate.

9. _____ (Indian) like chocolate.

10. _____ (Australian) like chocolate.

As well as using *the* + nationality adjective to generalise about all the people from a certain country, we can also use it to talk about a specific group of people from a country. In this case, we use *the* in the normal way, when I think the listener understands which group I mean. Compare these two sentences:

- **The** British drink a lot of tea [British people in general].

- **The** British climbed the hill [a specific group of British people, and the listener knows which group I mean].

It is also possible to use *the* + plural nationality noun to talk in general about the people from that country. There's really very little difference in meaning from using 'no article' + plural nationality noun:

- (The) Americans like chocolate.

- (The) Indonesians like chocolate.

However, it's important to note that if we say (for example) 'Canadians', we must mean all Canadians, Canadians in general. But, if we say 'the Canadians', it can mean Canadians in general, but it can also mean a specific group of Canadians that the listener knows about (in the same way as *the* + nationality adjective above):

- **Ø** Canadians are used to cold weather [Canadian people in general].

- **The** Canadians are used to cold weather [Canadian people in general].

But:

- **The** Canadians arrived [a specific group of Canadian people].

Section 3 Review Exercises

EXERCISE 3.6

Choose *the* or 'no article' (Ø).

1. I love _____ ice cream.

2. We were reading about _____ philosophy of the Middle Ages.

3. I really hate _____ cats on this street.

4. Look at _____ dust on this table!

5. She studied _____ fifteenth-century art.

6. The lecture was about _____ French literature.

7. She loves _____ ice cream that her mother makes.

8. David is allergic to _____ dust.

9. The children are keen on _____ animals.

10. We spent the afternoon learning about _____ novels of the twentieth century.

11. _____ cigarettes aren't allowed in here.

12. Could you please pass me _____ salt on the table?

13. She loves reading about _____ Chinese philosophy.

14. I don't like _____ animals that my brother has.

15. My mother really hates _____ cats.

16. He talks a lot about _____ art of the fourteenth century.

17. I'm not keen on _____ cheese.

18. Julie loves working with _____ children.

19. Where are _____ keys that I left in the hall?

20. We studied _____ African music.

EXERCISE 3.7

Choose *the* or 'no article' (Ø).

1. Can you teach me about _____ Italian food?

2. _____ flowers in that garden are very beautiful.

3. They learned about _____ twentieth-century theatre.

4. I really love _____ coffee.

5. _____ cakes that my flatmate makes are delicious.

6. _____ young people often have trouble finding jobs these days.

7. _____ money doesn't always lead to _____ happiness.

8. She wrote a book about _____ philosophy of the Middle Ages.

9. _____ peace is better than _____ war.

10. My brother likes _____ chocolate very much.

11. She wrote her thesis about _____ art of the nineteenth century.

12. Many people say that _____ teenagers are lazy, but I don't think that's true.

13. Please pass me _____ money on the table.

14. Julie likes _____ coffee that they serve in the café next to her house.

15. I like _____ children who live next door to my house – they are adorable.

16. He really hates _____ mushrooms.

17. _____ teenagers that I know all study hard.

18. We shouldn't take _____ good health for granted.

19. Could you give John _____ books that I left at your flat?

20. _____ Spanish usually go to bed later than _____ British.

EXERCISE 3.8

Choose *the* or 'no article' (Ø).

1. Julian says that politicians are too hard on _____ poor.

2. _____ Japanese often eat a very healthy diet.

3. She loves _____ Asian food.

4. This charity tries to help _____ hungry in poor countries.

5. How can we provide opportunities for _____ uneducated?

6. _____ Chinese often like green tea.

7. Many processed foods contain _____ palm oil.

8. Are _____ cars a problem?

9. He thinks _____ rich should pay more tax.

10. The Prime Minister is trying to help _____ unemployed.

11. _____ elderly are very powerful politically.

12. She doesn't drink _____ white wine.

13. _____ black clothes are popular in northern Europe.

14. She thought _____ people of Cambridge were extremely friendly.

15. I really like eating _____ spicy food.

16. This new hotel will be very popular with _____ tourist.

17. _____ rats can carry disease.

18. In the twenty-first century, _____ employees often work at home.

19. How will this new law affect _____ shopkeeper?

20. _____ young children need a lot of sleep.

(Remember that you can download all the exercises as printable PDFs at www.perfect-english-grammar.com/a-and-the.html.)

Section 4: Using *The* To Talk About Abstract Ideas

As we saw in Section 3, if we want to generalise using 'no article' we need to use a plural noun or an uncountable noun. On the other hand, sometimes we can use *the* + singular noun to talk about a whole category. In these cases, we are thinking about the category as a general abstract idea. In a sense, these are things which everybody knows, so we can use *the*.

Many of these words can be used as normal nouns as well. So we can say (for example) 'I like going to the library', meaning any library, the abstract idea of a library, but we can also use *the library / a library / libraries* in the normal way. So 'I'm going to the library today' might mean that I'm thinking about a specific library (for example, the library near my house, and I use *the* because the listener knows which library I mean). Or, I might be talking about the abstract idea of a library (and I haven't decided yet which one to go to). We can decide from the situation if the person talking means 'the library' in general or a specific library (or cinema / pub / gym and so on) but usually it doesn't matter.

Part 4.1: *The* with entertainment and recreation

We often use *the* to talk about entertainment as a general idea. Words used like this include:

the cinema	I often go to **the** cinema.
the opera	She loves **the** opera.
the ballet	I went to **the** ballet yesterday.
the theatre	He goes to **the** theatre at least twice a month.
the gym	Julie's gone to **the** gym.
the park	Shall we go to **the** park? It's such a lovely day.

the zoo	Elizabeth has never been to **the** zoo before!
the library	I must go to **the** library today! I really need to study.

Part 4.2: *The* with shops and other businesses

In the same way, we often use *the* with shops and businesses.

the baker's	Can't you buy bread at **the** baker's?
the bank	You should put your extra money in **the** bank.
the dentist's	I must go to **the** dentist's – I've got such a toothache.
the doctor's	She went to **the** doctor's yesterday.
the hairdresser's	He needs to go to **the** hairdresser's.
the post office	You can change money at **the** post office.
the pub	Let's go to **the** pub tonight.

(Strangely, however, we don't use *the café* or *the restaurant* in this way: 'let's go to **the** restaurant tonight' can only mean that I'm thinking about a specific restaurant. If I'm talking about the idea of a restaurant, I have to say 'let's go to **a** restaurant tonight'.)

Part 4.3: *The* with musical instruments

We usually use *the* when we are talking about musical instruments (and again we mean any piano, for example, not one particular one). The verb in this case is usually *play*:

- John plays **the** piano beautifully.
- Have you ever learned to play **the** guitar?

In US English, 'no article' is occasionally used with musical instruments.

Part 4.4: *The* with transport

First, we often use *the* when we are talking about a form of transport as a general idea. We usually do this with public transport (not with cars or bikes) and we usually use verbs such as *take, be on, get on* and *get off*:

the bus	We took **the** bus to school.
the underground / metro / subway	She gets off **the** underground in central London.
the plane	It's best to take **the** plane to New York City.
the train	Julie's on **the** train at the moment.
the boat / ferry	You can take **the** ferry to France.

In all of these examples, I'm not talking about a particular bus, train or plane but rather the system of transport as an idea. In the same way as the other nouns in this section, we can also use *a bus* (for example) in the normal way, when we are talking about any bus. If we use *the bus* it seems like we are talking about the whole system of public bus transport. Sometimes, there's really no difference in meaning between 'I'll get **a** bus' and 'I'll get **the** bus'.

We often use *the* with the places we go to get transport as well:

the airport	What time does her plane arrive at **the** airport?
the (train) station	Shall I give you a lift to **the** station?
the bus station	Do I need to go to **the** bus station to buy my ticket?
the bus stop	I was waiting at **the** bus stop when it started to rain.

If we use the name of the airport or station, then it's a proper noun and takes 'no article'. (See Part 9.3.1 for more about this). For example:

- I went to **the** airport to pick up my sister.
- What time do you need to be at **the** train station?

but

- She arrived at Ø Heathrow airport.

- I'll come and get you at Ø Euston Station.

However, we use 'no article' when we use a form of transport with *by*:

by car*	We travelled by Ø car.
by bus	He goes to work by Ø bus.
by underground / metro / subway	I went home by Ø underground.
by plane	I hate travelling by Ø plane.
by train	We went to Scotland by Ø train.
by taxi*	I love going by Ø taxi.
by bike*	He gets around London by Ø bike.
by motorbike*	The parcels were delivered by Ø motorbike.
by boat / by ferry	We went by Ø boat to France.

*We don't use *the car, the bike, the taxi* or *the motorbike* in the same way as the others. They are normal nouns.

Remember, we can't say '~~by foot~~' or '~~by feet~~' when we're talking about walking. We say 'on foot' (also 'no article').

EXERCISE 4.1

Fill the gap with *the* or 'no article' (Ø).

1. We travelled by _____ boat when we went on holiday.

2. Laura is on _____ train.

3. How do you get to work? On _____ foot?

4. Can I take _____ train to San Francisco?

5. Get off _____ subway at Central Park North.

6. She went to Paris by _____ train.

7. He loves travelling by _____ bike.

8. You shouldn't talk loudly while you're on _____ bus.

9. She could take _____ plane to Glasgow.

10. I travel around London by _____ bus.

Part 4.5: *The* with communication and media

We sometimes use a noun like *radio* with *the* to mean the whole system of communication in general, rather than just the object which you use:

the telephone / phone	Julie is on **the** phone.
the radio	We often listen to **the** radio.
the newspapers / the newspaper	**The** newspapers exposed the politician.
the post (UK) the mail (USA)	Has **the** post arrived yet? **The** mail usually comes about 10 a.m.

However, with *television* (and *TV*), we tend to use 'no article' for the abstract idea and *the* for the physical set:

- JOHN: What's on Ø television tonight? LUCY: There's a black and white film or a documentary about lions.

- We hung **the** television on the wall opposite the sofa.

In a similar way to transport, we use 'no article' when we use different kinds of communication with *by*:

by telephone / phone	We usually communicate by Ø phone.
by radio	The news was broadcast by Ø radio.
by mail (US) by post (UK)	The leaflets were sent by Ø mail. The cheques are coming by Ø post.
By email*	I sent the document by Ø email.

*We don't use *the email* in the same way as the others. *Email* is a normal noun.

EXERCISE 4.2

Fill the gap with the or 'no article' (Ø).

1. She sent the information by _____ email.

2. Did you hear the news on _____ radio?

3. Could you find out the time of the train by _____ phone?

4. The book arrived by _____ post.

5. Has _____ mail already arrived?

6. How much time do you spend on _____ phone?

7. The scandal was all over _____ newspapers.

8. Could we advertise by _____ mail?

9. These days news is communicated on the internet and the TV as well as by _____ radio.

10. Your document's in _____ post.

Part 4.6: *The* with inventions

We sometimes use *the* with singular countable nouns to talk in general about inventions and technology. This is optional and we often prefer to use 'no article' plus a plural or uncountable noun instead:

- **The** wheel was probably invented around 10,000 years ago.
- I think **the** computer has caused the biggest change recently in how we work.

Part 4.7: *The* with parts of the body

We usually use a possessive (like *my* or *his*) before parts of the body:
- I've hurt **my** leg.
- He broke **his** arm when he was skiing.

However, in the same way as with inventions, it's possible to use *the* to talk in general about parts of the body. This really has the same meaning as using 'no article' with a plural countable noun, as we saw in Section 3. This is most often used in formal English or scientific writing:

- **The** brain uses a lot of energy [= brains use a lot of energy].
- **The** heart needs exercise to stay healthy [= hearts need exercise to stay healthy.

We also occasionally use *the* with parts of the body after a preposition. This only happens after certain verbs (including *touch, shoot, take, pull, hit, kick, pat, grab, hold*, and *kiss*) and is almost like using a fixed phrase (see Section 8 for more about fixed phrases):

- She touched him on **the** arm [= she touched his arm].
- The criminal shot the policeman in **the** leg .
- Adam took his son by **the** hand.

EXERCISE 4.3

Julie is with her young son. Put in *his* or *the*.

1. Julie kissed _____ cheek.

2. Julie kissed him on _____ cheek.

3. Julie held _____ arm.

4. Julie held him by _____ arm.

5. Julie patted him on _____ back.

6. Julie patted _____ back.

Part 4.8: *The* with plants and animals

We can also use *the* + singular countable noun with plants and animals when we are talking about the whole species. This is most often used in formal writing. In the same way as with inventions (Part 4.6) and parts of the body (Part 4.7), the meaning is the same as 'no article' + plural noun:

- **The** snow leopard is in danger of becoming extinct [= snow leopards are …].
- **The** elephant is still hunted in many places for its tusks [= elephants are …].

Again, we can also use *the* + singular countable noun in the normal way – to talk about a specific animal that the listener knows about:

- **The** snow leopard at the zoo is pregnant.

Part 4.9: *The* with dances

We use *the* with some dances to talk about the dance as a general idea:

- *the tango*   **The** tango originated in Argentina.
- *the waltz*   She's learning to dance **the** waltz.
- *the foxtrot*   We did **the** foxtrot all night.

Part 4.10: *The* with geographical expressions

We also often use *the* with geographical expressions such as *the sea*, *the land*, *the country* and *the city*. Again, we use *the* to talk about the idea of 'the city' or 'the country' and not about a particular place:

the city	I like living in **the** city because there's so much to do.
the sea	I love **the** sea.
the mountains	We prefer to go to **the** mountains on holiday.
the beach	He often goes to **the** beach.
the country / the countryside	We went to **the** country(side) for the weekend.
the seaside	In the old days, people used to go to **the** seaside for their holidays.

In the same way as with the other nouns in this section, we can often use these nouns as normal nouns (though this is not true for *seaside* or *countryside*):

- She lives in **a** city in the north of England. [In this case, I'm talking about a particular city, but one which the listener doesn't know, so I use *a*.]

Part 4.11: *The* with weather

We sometimes use *the* with different kinds of weather, to talk about the general idea of rain, fog, snow, etc.:

the wind	The sounds of **the** wind makes me feel cold!
the rain	I don't mind **the** rain.
the snow	It can be dangerous to drive in **the** snow.
the fog	In **the** fog, London looks like a scene from a novel by Dickens.
the sunshine	I love sitting in **the** sunshine.

We also use *the* with the word *weather*:

- What's **the** weather like in June?

However, we also often use these weather words as normal nouns. So, we can also use *the* to talk about a particular piece of weather that the listener knows about:

- She sat in **the** sunshine that was streaming through her window.

Usually it really doesn't matter if we're talking about the general idea or a particular piece of weather:

- She sat in **the** sunshine. [This can mean either *sunshine* as a general idea or a particular piece of *sunshine* that the listener knows about. It really doesn't make any difference to the sentence.]

We can also use 'no article' if we mean a particular piece of weather that the listener doesn't know about.

- I left a bucket outside last night and in the morning it was full of Ø rain.

Sometimes there's very little difference in meaning, and you can choose *the* or 'no article':

- I could hear Ø rain on the roof all night.
- I could hear **the** rain on the roof all night.

Part 4.12: *The* with certain time words

We often use *the* with certain time words when we're talking in an abstract way:

the morning	I like drinking coffee in **the** morning.
the afternoon	But I like drinking tea in **the** afternoon.
the evening	I met her in **the** evening.
the day / daytime	I don't work in **the** daytime; instead I do all my work in the evening.
the night	He's often awake for most of **the** night.
the week	She's at university during **the** week.
the weekend	At **the** weekend, I love to sleep late.

However, there are some fixed expressions like *at night* and *by night / by day* that take 'no article':

- She doesn't like walking home at Ø night.
- By Ø day the park is very busy; by Ø night it's empty.

See Part 6.2 for more about time words and expressions.

EXERCISE 4.4

Fill the gap with *the* or 'no article' (Ø).

1. What time do you get up in _____ morning?

2. By _____ day he's an accountant, but after work he's the drummer in a rock group.

3. We usually study in _____ afternoon.

4. They often go to the pub at _____ night.

5. I'm sorry, I can't meet during _____ week. I'm very busy at work at the moment.

6. By _____ night, London looks totally different.

7. He works during _____ day.

8. What are you doing at _____ weekend?

9. She met her friends in _____ evening.

10. It's so cold here! Even in _____ daytime, it's below freezing.

Part 4.13: *The* with grammatical expressions

We often use *the* with the names of tenses and other grammatical expressions:

the present simple (tense)	Put these sentences into **the** present simple.
the past (tense)	Why did you use **the** past tense here?
the future perfect (tense)	What does **the** future perfect mean?

Part 4.14: Other words with *the*

the past	It must have been difficult to live without electricity in **the** past.
the future	Can you imagine what life will be like in **the** future?
the present	There's no time like **the** present.
the internet	I looked the word up on **the** internet.
the web	Let's check the answer on **the** web.
the environment	We need to think about protecting **the** environment.
the climate	**The** climate is getting warmer.
the press	Should **the** press be regulated by the government?
the public	Is this castle open to **the** public?
the police	Call **the** police! There's been a robbery!
the fire brigade	**The** fire brigade arrived extremely quickly.

Part 4.15: Words which are not like this

There are some words which logically we feel should be like the words above, but they aren't. Be careful! These words are normal nouns (and are mostly uncountable). We use *the* only when the listener knows which one we mean (for example because we say so in the rest of the sentence) and we use 'no article' when we are talking in general. In the examples below, I'm using these words in general, so I use 'no article' (as we saw in Section 3). So we say, for instance, 'I love nature' and not 'I love the nature'.

nature	I love Ø nature.
society	We need to consider problems in Ø society.
space	She's always dreamed about travelling into Ø space.
pollution	How can we reduce Ø pollution?
life	Ø Life can be hard!
technology	How do you think Ø technology will change our lives?
history	He wrote a book about Ø history.
philosophy	I love studying Ø philosophy.
science	Are you interested in Ø science?
literature	Ø Literature is important for young people.
art	She is keen on Ø art.
music	He often listens to Ø music.
poverty	We should all try to fight Ø poverty.
crime	Ø Crime is a real problem in this city.
unemployment	Ø Unemployment is increasing.
global warming	How can we stop Ø global warming?
luck	It was Ø luck that helped her to pass the exam.
climate change*	Everybody is talking about Ø climate change these days.

'A' AND 'THE' EXPLAINED • 55

* But we say '**the** climate' (see Part 4.14; see also Part 7.1 for noun adjuncts).

See also Part 3.2.1 about using words such as *history* and *music* with modification.

Section 4 Review Exercises

EXERCISE 4.5

Choose *the* or 'no article' (Ø).

1. She works for _____ fire brigade.

2. We travelled by _____ plane.

3. I really need a holiday at _____ beach!

4. _____ pollution is a major problem in our cities.

5. Shall we go to _____ cinema tonight?

6. I'd love to go to _____ opera.

7. Young people don't know enough about _____ literature.

8. He's worried about _____ crime.

9. She caught _____ train at King's Cross station.

10. The boss said he would contact Julie by _____ phone.

11. We met at _____ pub.

12. Lucy can play _____ violin beautifully.

13. I took _____ bus to the concert.

14. I need to take my son to _____ doctor's today, so I can't come to lunch.

15. I went to the party by _____ car.

16. My grandmother refuses to put her money in _____ bank.

17. I'll send you the bill by _____ email.

18. I love listening to my husband play _____ cello.

19. I can't meet you in _____ week, as I always work late.

20. She went from Warsaw to London by _____ bus.

EXERCISE 4.6

Choose *the* or 'no article' (Ø).

1. I really love listening to _____ music.

2. She studies _____ philosophy at university.

3. John has played _____ piano since he was a child.

4. She went to _____ ballet on her birthday.

5. Do you like _____ city?

6. He hates swimming in _____ sea, and prefers a swimming pool.

7. Are you interested in _____ art?

8. _____ poverty is the biggest problem we need to solve.

9. I bought some bread at _____ baker's.

10. My cousin is sometimes on _____ radio talking about the economy.

11. I took lessons to learn how to play _____ clarinet.

12. To succeed as a writer you need _____ luck and good timing.

13. It's easy to get around Paris by _____ metro.

14. The parcel will come by _____ post.

15. They often visit _____ theatre.

16. You can take _____ underground to the restaurant.

17. I spent two hours on _____ phone last night.

18. There was a programme about _____ climate change on TV last night.

19. Listen to _____ wind!

20. She loves _____ nature and often goes for long walks in the country.

EXERCISE 4.7

Choose *the* or 'no article' (Ø).

1. She sent the invitation in _____ post.

2. Lucy went for a swim, and then to _____ hairdresser's.

3. We might take _____ boat to France.

4. I'm not rich enough to always travel by _____ taxi!

5. Responsibility is important for _____ society.

6. If you have toothache, you should go to _____ dentist's.

7. You can exchange money at _____ post office.

8. We often go to _____ seaside in summer.

9. My mother lives in _____ countryside.

10. It's important to keep up with _____ technology.

11. I love going to university by _____ bike.

12. The satellite is in _____ space.

13. He travelled around the USA by _____ motorbike.

14. I went skiing in _____ mountains.

15. We usually drink tea at around four o'clock in _____ afternoon.

16. _____ life can be difficult when you don't have much money.

17. London looks much better in _____ sunshine.

18. She travelled around Japan by _____ train.

19. _____ unemployment has risen recently.

20. We learned about _____ global warming at school.

EXERCISE 4.8

Choose *the* or 'no article' (Ø).

1. She hates _____ city and much prefers to live in a village.

2. How does the government's attitude affect _____ society?

3. She can't come for coffee because she has to go to _____ doctor's.

4. I'd love to live by _____ sea.

5. He explored Argentina by _____ motorbike.

6. Do you spend a lot of time on _____ phone?

7. It's important to be happy in _____ present.

8. My mother thinks I should put all my money in my savings account at _____ bank.

9. In Cambridge, everyone gets around by _____ bike.

10. He listens to _____ radio every night.

11. He's interested in _____ nature and the environment.

12. I really hate going to _____ dentist's.

13. Would you like to travel into _____ space?

14. Shall we go to _____ library later?

15. He plays _____ piano very well.

16. They travelled from England to Spain by _____ boat.

17. Do you go to work on _____ foot?

18. We went hiking in _____ mountains on holiday.

19. How often do you go to _____ hairdresser's?

20. I need to buy some stamps at _____ post office.

EXERCISE 4.9

Choose *the* or 'no article' (Ø).

1. We travelled around Tokyo by _____ underground.

2. Do you often work in _____ evening?

3. She often gets up for a glass of water during _____ night.

4. John needs a new tie because he's going to _____ opera.

5. He goes to work by _____ car.

6. The children love _____ seaside.

7. I'd love to visit Brazil in _____ future.

8. We went for a walk and enjoyed _____ sunshine.

9. She lay in bed and listened to _____ wind outside.

10. _____ unemployment is a big problem at the moment.

11. She travelled around California by _____ bus.

12. His grandfather thinks that _____ climate change is a myth.

13. What shall we do tomorrow? How about going to _____ zoo?

14. The children learn a lot about _____ global warming.

15. He likes getting up early and walking to _____ baker's to buy fresh bread.

16. I often go to Scotland by _____ plane, although occasionally I drive.

17. She loves playing _____ violin.

18. Many companies are trying to reduce _____ pollution.

19. Can your brother play _____ guitar?

20. How can we tackle _____ poverty?

EXERCISE 4.10

Choose *the* or 'no article' (Ø).

1. The bill will come in _____ post.

2. Did you take _____ bus home yesterday?

3. You need _____ luck and skill to win.

4. How often do you go to _____ cinema?

5. He usually takes _____ plane when he goes to Paris.

6. How can we use _____ technology to improve everybody's life?

7. A friend of mine took _____ train all the way across Russia.

8. I need an exercise about _____ future tense.

9. She loves going to _____ theatre.

10. I try not to sleep in _____ daytime.

11. She spends a lot of time listening to _____ music.

12. We often go to _____ ballet.

13. Last week, we went to a lecture about _____ history.

14. That's _____ life!

15. She loves _____ beach and takes a holiday by the Mediterranean at least twice a year.

16. We studied _____ present perfect tense in my English class today.

17. She sent the money by _____ post.

18. His brother plays _____ piano beautifully.

19. She really knows how to dance _____ tango.

20. How will _____ public react to this new law?

EXERCISE 4.11

Choose *the* or 'no article' (Ø).

1. We did _____ foxtrot all night.

2. Did you come by _____ taxi?

3. He usually goes to work by _____ underground.

4. I like to get up early in _____ morning.

5. The Prime Minister promised to reduce _____ crime.

6. What do you like to do at _____ weekend?

7. Can you imagine what it was like to live in _____ past? No electricity, no mobile phones, no running water!

8. He studied _____ history at university.

9. Tim Berners-Lee invented _____ World Wide Web in the 1980s.

10. They try to recycle as much as possible as it's good for _____ environment.

11. What's _____ weather like in Australia at the moment?

12. I really like _____ climate here – not too hot, not too cold.

13. Celebrities often have a love/hate relationship with _____ press.

14. Most British people trust _____ police.

15. She learned _____ waltz at school.

16. I usually read _____ newspaper on Sundays.

17. The government is reducing the money it gives to _____ science.

18. I'll be in touch by _____ email.

19. We often go to _____ countryside for the weekend.

20. Please write your essay in _____ past tense.

(Remember that you can download all the exercises as printable PDFs at www.perfect-english-grammar.com/a-and-the.html.)

Section 5: Using 'A/An' To Talk About Members Of Categories

Part 5.1: Explanation

5.1.1 Using one member of a category to generalise

In Section 3, we saw that it's possible to use *a/an + singular countable noun* to talk about one member of a group or category. We can use this member as a way of generalising about the whole category. It's as if we take one member as an example. Anything which is true for this member is true for the whole group.

- **A** child needs love.

This really means the same as when we use 'no article' + plural or uncountable noun to generalise about all the members of a group or category.

- Ø Children need love.

In both these cases we are talking about children in general.

5.1.2 Using one member of a category to mean 'it doesn't matter which'

It's also possible to use *a/an* + singular countable noun to talk about any member of a group or category. This time, we're not generalising about the whole group, but instead saying that it doesn't matter or we don't know which one (or ones) we are talking about. If we use 'no article' + plural or uncountable noun then we mean a certain amount of the members of the category.

- I need **a** cup of coffee.

In this case, I'm not generalising about cups of coffee. Instead, I'm saying that I need one cup and it doesn't matter which one. Any cup of coffee is good! In this case, when we make the noun plural, it doesn't mean the whole category. Instead, it means 'some' or 'a certain number':

- We all need Ø cups of coffee.

The same thing is true when we use an uncountable noun. We're talking about 'some' or 'a certain amount':

- Could you buy Ø milk?

In Section 2 we studied using *the* when both the speaker and the listener know which particular thing or set of things is being talked about, and using *a/an* or 'no article' when the speaker knows which one(s) but the listener doesn't. However, sometimes neither the speaker nor the listener knows which specific noun is being talked about. Instead, the speaker is talking about any member of a certain group or category. It's not important to know exactly which member. We still use *a/an* (for singular countable nouns) or 'no article' (for plural or uncountable nouns), because the listener doesn't know which one(s). For example, with *a/an*:

- I'd like **a** cup of tea. [The speaker doesn't know which one, neither does the listener. It doesn't matter which particular cup of tea.]

- I need to see **a** doctor. [Any doctor; neither the listener nor the speaker is thinking about a particular doctor.]

- Could you pass me **a** pen please? [Any pen, the speaker doesn't know which one.]

And with 'no article':

- I'd like Ø chips.

- Could you buy Ø milk later, please?

- Lucy's job is looking after Ø children.

(With plural or uncountable nouns, we often use *some*. See Appendix 3.)

We use *a/an* and 'no article' in the same way with hypothetical things (that is, when we're talking about the idea of something but we don't know if it really exists). Again, the listener doesn't know which one and neither does the speaker. They're just imagining a situation. This is often the case with questions. As the listener doesn't know which thing or group of things the speaker has in mind, we use *a/an* for singular countable nouns and 'no article' for uncountable nouns and plural nouns. For example:

- We need **a** secretary who speaks German and Italian. [I don't know if this kind of secretary exists. Neither the speaker nor the listener know which particular secretary, so we use *a*.]

- Is there **a** tall girl in your class?
- She wants Ø new shoes.

EXERCISE 5.1

Choose *the* if the listener knows or can guess which particular noun or nouns. Choose *a/an* or 'no article' if it doesn't matter which example of a noun.

1. I'm going to buy Julie _____ cake for her birthday.

2. I always go to _____ café around the corner from our house. You know the one.

3. Could you try to find me _____ new saucepan when you're at the shops?

4. What happened to the rest of _____ soup that we ate yesterday?

5. We'd like _____ large bottle of orange juice, please.

6. _____ water in my house is really brown!

7. Pass me _____ spoon next to your hand, please.

8. I'm looking for _____ job.

9. If I were you, I'd take _____ taxi to the airport.

10. Could you lend me _____ pen?

11. Do you know _____ good dentist?

12. Is there _____ park near here?

13. That child looks really cold. She needs _____ coat.

14. This is _____ plant that I told you about. Isn't it beautiful?

15. I wish I lived in _____ house by the sea.

Part 5.2: Classifying and describing people or things

We use *a/an* (for singular nouns) and 'no article' (for plural or uncountable nouns) when we're using members of categories to describe or classify people or things:

- The film was **a** comedy.
- Sage is **a** herb.

- His laptop is **a** PC.
- She's **a** lovely girl.
- 'What are these?' 'They're **Ø** cakes'.
- John and Lucy are **Ø** lively children.
- Oxford and Bath are **Ø** cities in England.

This includes people's jobs:

- Julie is **a** teacher [= she is part of the group which includes all teachers].
- John works as **an** accountant.
- I'm **a** student.

We don't usually use 'no article' with singular nouns if they are jobs or professions ('~~Julie is teacher~~', '~~John works as accountant~~', '~~I'm student~~'), though see Part 6.5 about when a job is a unique role.

Again, if we want to use a plural noun, we need 'no article':

- John and Susan are **Ø** teachers.
- We are **Ø** accountants.

Here are some more examples using *a/an* with other categories of people. In this case, it's religious, ethical and political beliefs:

- She's **a** vegetarian [= she is a member of the group of vegetarians in the world].
- He's **a** Muslim.

With a plural noun, we use 'no article':

- They are **Ø** socialists.
- Many European people are **Ø** Catholics.

We often use *a/an* with singular countable nouns when we describe something using a verb such as *look like* or *sound like* (or other verbs used for describing), or the preposition *as*:

- She looks like **a** dancer.

- He used his knife as **a** screwdriver.
- That sounds like **a** car outside.

With singular uncountable nouns or plural nouns we use 'no article':

- This coffee tastes like **Ø** mud.
- The boys in the choir sound like **Ø** angels.

Remember, we generally can't use a singular countable noun alone (except in special situations, like after *a sort of* – see below), so we must use *a/an* in the following situations:

- He's **a** teacher [not 'He's teacher'].
- The film is **a** drama [not 'The film is drama'].
- He looks like **an** athlete [not 'He looks like athlete'].

However, we don't usually use an article (in UK English) after *a kind of, a sort of, a type of* or *a variety of*:

- He's a sort of **Ø** journalist.
- Chai is a kind of **Ø** tea.
- Samba is a type of **Ø** music.
- Peppermint is a variety of **Ø** mint.

Be careful! *An example of* is NOT like this:

- That's a good example of **a** correct sentence.

EXERCISE 5.2

Fill the gap with *a/an* or 'no article' (Ø).

1. She's _____ lawyer.

2. That sounds like _____ lorry outside.

3. Dr Seuss is _____ children's book.

4. Maria and Juan are _____ engineers.

5. A Ferrari is a kind of _____ car.

6. Korma is _____ Indian dish.

7. Julia works as _____ waitress.

8. My nephew looked like _____ old man when he was born.

9. Basil is a variety of _____ herb.

10. A barrister is a sort of _____ lawyer.

11. That car is _____ Mercedes.

12. They are _____ very nice people.

13. Noriko and Kumiko are _____ students.

14. David is _____ professor.

15. What's in this box? It looks like _____ chocolate!

16. I work as _____ teacher.

17. That sounds like _____ bell.

18. Reggae is a kind of _____ music.

19. My sisters are _____ doctors.

20. Elizabeth is _____ extremely intelligent girl.

Part 5.3: Exclamations

We often use exclamations to categorise something or someone. With *what* + singular countable nouns we need *a/an*. If the noun is uncountable or plural, we use 'no article'.

What a/an + singular countable nouns:

- What **a** beautiful day!
- What **a** party!
- What **a** horrible taste!

What + plural or uncountable nouns:

- What **Ø** terrible weather!

- What Ø lovely shoes!
- What Ø luck!

EXERCISE 5.3

Fill the gap with *a/an* or 'no article' (Ø).

1. What _____ cute baby!

2. What _____ fun!

3. What _____ heavy rain!

4. What _____ day!

5. What _____ fantastic music!

6. What _____ warm evening!

7. What _____ beautiful clothes!

8. What _____ horrible journey!

9. What _____ interesting book!

10. What _____ traffic!

Section 5 Review Exercises

EXERCISE 5.4

Choose *a/an* or 'no article'(Ø).

1. Lucy is _____ lawyer.

2. What _____ awful weather!

3. They looked like _____ thieves.

4. John and Susan are _____ Christians.

5. Does that farm sell _____ eggs?

6. This is a sort of _____ magazine.

7. What _____ delicious cakes!

8. She's looking for _____ Japanese teacher.

9. I need _____ cup of tea!

10. Could you pass me _____ glass?

11. Do you know _____ cheap restaurant near here?

12. We need _____ music!

13. Could you buy _____ pasta when you're at the shop?

14. Emma's at the market looking for _____ brown rice.

15. Are there _____ plants in your office?

16. This garden needs _____ grass!

17. What _____ lovely holiday!

18. Julie and Luke are _____ nurses.

19. I want _____ new cushions for my living room.

20. Do you have _____ lemonade?

EXERCISE 5.5

Choose *a/an* or 'no article'(Ø).

1. John works as _____ accountant.

2. What _____ ugly car!

3. What _____ tasty meal!

4. Several of my friends are _____ vegetarians.

5. What _____ fantastic prize!

6. What _____ interesting buildings!

7. I'd like to be _____ surgeon when I've finished university.

8. Espresso is a kind of _____ coffee.

9. That sounds like _____ water.

10. What _____ lovely food!

11. They advertised for _____ receptionists who know Spanish, German and Portuguese.

12. He'd like _____ new clothes.

13. She's _____ actress.

14. Yoshi and Yuka are _____ Buddhists.

15. That's a kind of _____ cake.

16. What _____ horrible story!

17. Richard's _____ taxi driver.

18. What _____ beautiful shoes!

19. My parents are _____ police officers.

20. I'd love _____ bigger house.

(Remember that you can download all the exercises as printable PDFs at www.perfect-english-grammar.com/a-and-the.html.)

Section 6: Words That Generally Have 'No Article'

Part 6.1: Languages, meals and sports

6.1.1 Languages

We generally use 'no article' with languages:

- She speaks Ø Japanese [not 'She speaks the Japanese'].

- They're studying Ø Spanish [not 'They're studying the Spanish'].

Notice that the word *language* itself isn't in this category! It's a normal noun. So we say '**the** language that I speak at home' or 'she's learning **a** new language'.

6.1.2 Meals

In general, we use 'no article' with the names of meals such as *breakfast, dinner, lunch, supper, tea*:

- What shall we have for Ø dinner?

- What time do you usually have Ø lunch?

- I didn't eat Ø breakfast this morning.

6.1.3 Sports

Sports usually have 'no article':

- I don't like Ø golf.

- He often plays Ø tennis.

- We practised Ø judo for many years.

- Ø Baseball is popular in Japan.
- John loves playing Ø rugby.

6.1.4 Using these words in an unusual way

Usually, we use 'no article' with languages, sports and meals. However, if we are using these words in a slightly different way, then we can use *a/an* or *the*. Essentially, languages, sports and meals are usually exceptions to the rules about *the* and *a/an*. If we use these words in a different way from usual, then they stop being exceptions and we need to use all the rules that we've already talked about:

	Usual use	*Unusual use*
Languages	I speak Ø French, Ø English and Ø Spanish.	**The** French that they speak in Montreal is different from **the** French that they speak in Paris. He speaks **a** beautiful Spanish. [A particular kind of Spanish, which is beautiful.]
Meals	I had Ø lunch and went out. Let's have Ø dinner at eight.	(Often talking about a special occasion or with an adjective before the meal.) **The** lunch we had after the wedding was really excellent. There will be **a** dinner for her birthday. Let's have **an** early supper.
Sports	I love playing Ø football.	**The** football that they play in the USA is completely different from **the** football that we play in the UK.

Part 6.2: Time Words

Many time words and phrases have 'no article'.

(See also Part 7.11 for how to use *next* and *last* with time expressions, Part 4.12 for how to use *the* with some time words and Part 7.9.2 for clock times with *quarter* and *half*.)

6.2.1 Months

Generally we use 'no article' with months. We can use the tense of the rest of the sentence to understand which particular month we mean:

- I'll see you in Ø December [= next December].
- We met in Ø December [= last December].

6.2.2 Days of the week

These usually take 'no article'. In the same way as for months, we use the rest of the sentence to understand which particular day we mean:

- I'm meeting Julia on Ø Monday [= next Monday].
- I met Julia on Ø Monday [= last Monday].

Also:

- She started work last Ø Wednesday.
- He plays tennis every Ø Thursday.

We can also use 'no article' with plural days of the week to mean 'every':

- We have our Russian class on Ø Fridays.
- I work on Ø Mondays and Ø Tuesdays.

6.2.3 Holidays and special days

We generally use 'no article' with holidays:

- We usually eat turkey on Ø Christmas Day.
- They went to watch the fireworks on Ø New Year's Eve.
- Do you fast during Ø Ramadan?
- On Ø Mother's Day, I sent my mum some flowers.
- Children like to eat chocolate at Ø Halloween.

6.2.4 Dates

With dates we use *the* if the date has the number first (most common in British English):

- We got married on **the** 22nd of September.

We use 'no article' if the date has the number second (most common in US English):

- She met him on Ø November 16th.

6.2.5 Parts of the day

We also use 'no article' when we're talking about parts of a day (morning, afternoon, evening, night), if we say the name of the day:

- On Wednesday Ø night we went to the theatre.
- I met John on Friday Ø morning.

See Part 4.12 for more information about using *the* with parts of the day.

6.2.6 Seasons

We can use either *the* or 'no article' when we talk about seasons:

- Where's **the** spring?
- She always goes to Spain in Ø summer.
- I don't go to the park very often in **the** winter.
- Ø Autumn is my favourite season.

While it's possible to use 'no article' with *fall* (in US English), it's more common to use *the*:

- I love all the beautiful colours in **the** fall.

6.2.7 Years, decades, centuries and historical periods

We use 'no article' with years:

- She was born in Ø 1991.
- This castle was built in Ø 1672.

We use *the* with centuries:

- Shakespeare was born in **the** sixteenth century.
- People started living in this area in **the** 1700s.

We use *the* with decades:

- The Beatles were popular in **the** 1960s.

- I first became interested in music in **the** eighties.

We use *the* with historical periods:

- Michelangelo was working during **the** Renaissance.
- What was life like in **the** Middle Ages?

6.2.8 Using these words in an unusual way

In the same way as with languages, meals and sports, we can use the time words above in an unusual way. In this case, they might need a different article.

Normal use:

- Let's meet on Ø Monday [= next Monday].
- My birthday is in Ø June.
- I visit my family at Ø Christmas.

Unusual use:

- Do you remember **the** Monday when we met? [A particular Monday that you know.]
- **The** June when we got married was the hottest for years.
- We stayed at home for **the** Christmas when Lucy was born.

With seasons, normally we can choose *the* or 'no article' (as discussed above), but if we want to emphasise the fact that we're talking about a particular summer (for example), we need *the*:

- I really improved my French **the** summer that we went to France.

Finally, we can also use *a* with days of the week, if we mean *any*:

- Could we meet on **a** Monday? I'm usually not busy then.

Part 6.3: Nouns followed by a classifying letter or number

When a noun has a number or letter after it, it doesn't usually take an article:

- Please write down your answer to Ø question 2.

- I found the quote on Ø page 197.
- She left her passport at Ø gate 18 by mistake.
- The train for Paris leaves from Ø platform 12.
- What's the answer to Ø number three?
- In Ø section two of the book, the author describes his life as a young man.
- Ring the doorbell of Ø flat 7. I think that's where they live.
- I went to Ø room 226 but it was empty. Has my class been moved?
- You can see how this works in Ø diagram 4, on the next page.
- Please read Ø part B of the book for homework, and we'll discuss it next week.
- I found all the information I needed in Ø section D of the report.
- All the students had problems with Ø question B. It was quite difficult.
- Which bus stop do we need? Ø Stop C or Ø Stop D?

An exception to this is when you are talking about the number or letter itself, for example when teaching a child to read. In this case, the number or letter is a normal noun:

- What's this number? It's **a** number four.
- Please write **a** letter 'D'. Next to **the** 'D', write **an** 'O'.

(We also often need *the* with the names of roads that include numbers, such as *the M8*. See Part 9.3.1.)

On the other hand, if we use ordinal numbers, such as *first* or *second*, before the noun, we usually need *the* (see Part 7.12 for more information):

- Our class will be held in **the** first room on the left.
- Please answer **the** second question.

EXERCISE 6.1

Fill the gap with *the* or 'no article' (Ø).

1. Could you tell me the answer to _____ question 6, please?

2. The trains from London arrive at _____ platform 7.

3. Her office is on _____ third floor.

4. John, could you read out _____ number three, please?

5. The description of the house is in _____ section eight of the book.

6. Could you pass me _____ first box on the right, please?

7. The diagram on _____ page 84 is not correct.

8. The classroom is on _____ second floor.

9. His flight leaves from _____ gate 18.

10. I don't know the answer to _____ eighth question.

11. The class will be held in _____ room 336.

12. We need to read _____ first part of the book for homework.

13. They live in _____ third flat.

14. The date of publication is normally on _____ first page of the book.

15. Please look at _____ diagram 23.

16. This is _____ first book I've ever read by this author.

17. Could you begin reading from the beginning of _____ part four?

18. They live in _____ flat 3.

19. Is this _____ first time that you've visited London?

20. She's _____ third person I've met this week who knows my sister!

Part 6.4: Newspaper headlines

It's sometimes possible to drop the articles in newspaper headlines:

- DOG ATTACKS POSTMAN

This is really the journalist's choice. It's not necessary to drop the articles. It also depends on the type of headline. Main headlines are more likely to drop articles, while subheadings and headlines which include quotes are much less likely to drop the articles.

If you decide to keep the first article, usually then all the articles are kept:

- **A** DOG ATTACKS **A** POSTMAN [not 'A DOG ATTACKS POSTMAN']

Part 6.5: Unique roles

Usually we use *a/an* with a person's job, but if there's only one of a certain role, and it's clear to the listener which role we're talking about, then it's possible to use *the*:

- Julie is **a** headteacher.
- Julie is **the** headteacher of our school.

What's more, in some special cases, we can use 'no article'. This is often true when the job is the only one of its kind in an organisation and we are using certain verbs, including *elect, appoint, become* and *be*:

- Julie was appointed Ø headteacher of our school.
- Julie became Ø headteacher of our school.
- Julie is Ø headteacher of our school.

However, we can do so in other situations too, and this can be understood as a type of fixed expression (see Section 8 for more about fixed expressions). The job title is not the subject of the sentence and is usually used after a verb such as *be*, *elect* or *appoint*, or after the preposition *as*. In all cases, it's clear to the listener which organisation is being talked about:

captain	John is Ø captain of the football team.
chairman	Mrs Brown was appointed Ø chairman of the charity.
CEO	Luke started working as Ø CEO last week [it's clear to the listener which company he is CEO of].
director	We elected Amy Ø director of the committee.
treasurer	He was appointed Ø treasurer.
king	He became Ø king in 1781.
queen	Elizabeth Windsor was crowned Ø queen in Westminster Abbey.

president	She was elected Ø president.
professor	He became Ø professor of sociology in 2012.
chief	She was made Ø chief of staff last year.
head	He was appointed Ø head of HR.

EXERCISE 6.2

Fill the gap with 'no article' if possible. Otherwise use *a/an*.

1. She was elected _____ president.

2. Catherine is _____ pilot.

3. I'm _____ bank clerk.

4. Adam is _____ CEO of our company.

5. Ellie was appointed _____ professor of philosophy at Oxford.

6. Mary was crowned _____ queen in 1543.

7. John works as _____ teacher.

8. Lucy's _____ lawyer.

9. He got a new job working as _____ shop assistant.

10. He became _____ treasurer in 2010.

Part 6.6: *Fact is*

Recently, I've often seen *the* dropped from *the fact is*, *the problem is* and *the question is* at the beginning of a sentence. This is more common in US English. You can choose either *the* or 'no article' with these expressions:

- (The) fact is, I just don't like mushrooms.

- (The) problem is, he's really not suited to his job.

- (The) question is, what should we do next?

- (The) truth is, I have no money left.

Section 6 Review Exercises

EXERCISE 6.3

If it's possible, put 'no article' (Ø). If not, put *the*.

1. Can you speak _____ Turkish?

2. This book is written in _____ Arabic.

3. What's the answer to _____ question ten?

4. _____ winter that Julie was born was cold and snowy.

5. Would you like to have _____ dinner at home or shall we go out?

6. Have you ever tried _____ judo?

7. Did I tell you about _____ delicious lunch that we had in Paris?

8. Elizabeth was elected _____ President of the United States.

9. He's studying _____ Spanish.

10. The party is on _____ third of February.

11. I learned _____ tennis at school.

12. I had _____ breakfast in a café yesterday.

13. What are you doing at _____ Christmas?

14. Could you write _____ question number four on the board, please?

15. She speaks _____ English fluently.

16. He cooked _____ most amazing dinner.

17. Would you like to go to the cinema on _____ Friday night?

18. _____ baseball is very popular in Japan.

19. Do you fast during _____ Ramadan?

20. Could you pass me _____ third book on the shelf, please?

EXERCISE 6.4

If it's possible, put 'no article' (Ø). If not, put *the*.

1. Do you remember _____ July when we met?

2. Shall we have coffee on _____ Monday?

3. Julie is studying _____ Japanese.

4. Could you come on _____ 6th of August?

5. The information about proper nouns is in _____ Section 9.

6. Do you play _____ rugby at school?

7. I love _____ summer!

8. She can speak _____ Spanish really well.

9. We often go on holiday in _____ May.

10. How about meeting on _____ Tuesday afternoon?

11. Please turn to _____ question D on your exam paper.

12. He was crowned _____ king in Westminster Abbey.

13. _____ fact is, I don't like tea very much, even though I'm British.

14. Her office is on _____ second floor.

15. I love _____ skiing.

16. _____ winter that I was in Japan was one of the best winters of my life.

17. Do you celebrate _____ Easter?

18. The train leaves from _____ platform 6.

19. _____ English that they speak in Glasgow is quite different from how people speak in London.

20. He was elected _____ Prime Minister.

(Remember that you can download all the exercises as printable PDFs at www.perfect-english-grammar.com/a-and-the.html.)

Section 7: Special Cases And Difficulties

Part 7.1: Noun adjuncts

In English, we're able to use two nouns together. The first noun (sometimes called a noun adjunct) gives us information about the second noun in the same way that an adjective does. For example:

- vegetable soup [the noun adjunct *vegetable* works as an adjective and gives us information about the main noun *soup*].

- world map [the noun adjunct *world* gives us information about *map*. *Map* is the main noun].

The important thing to notice about this kind of structure is that we think about the main noun (which comes second) when we choose the article. We don't think about the noun adjunct (which comes first).

For example, we usually use *the* with musical instruments, so we say 'she plays the piano'. But when we use *piano* as a noun adjunct, for example in 'piano lesson', then we need to think about *lesson* when we choose the article. *Lesson* is a normal noun. It doesn't always take *the*. It takes *a* or *the* or 'no article' depending on the situation. For example:

- She plays **the** piano.

But

- She's taking ∅ piano lessons [the listener doesn't know which particular lessons, and 'lessons' is plural, so we use 'no article'].

- I really hated **the** piano lesson I had yesterday [the listener knows which lesson because it's mentioned in the sentence, so we use *the*].

- He missed **a** piano lesson because his train was so late [the listener doesn't know exactly which lesson, and it's singular, so we use *a*].

More examples:

- 'I saw **the** sun' but 'She uses Ø sun cream every day'. [See also Part 2.3 about *the sun*.]

- 'I use **the** internet at work' but 'She asked her question in **an** internet forum'. [See also Part 4.14 about *the internet*.]

- 'They speak Ø French' but 'He bought **a** French dictionary'. [See also Part 6.1.1 about languages.]

EXERCISE 7.1

Choose the correct article.

1. Look at _____ sky! It's a beautiful shade of pink!

2. Neil Armstrong explored in _____ moon buggy.

3. Have you had _____ lunch yet?

4. She can play _____ guitar really well.

5. I think we should fix the roof properly now, so we can avoid _____ future problems.

6. The government needs to think more about protecting _____ environment.

7. We had _____ Russian lesson every Friday when I was at university.

8. The children made a model of _____ world.

9. John has _____ cough.

10. The children can't leave the classroom until _____ lunch bell rings.

11. She bought _____ new work outfit.

12. They are learning to speak _____ Russian.

13. He's working as _____ guitar teacher.

14. Mary bought _____ cough medicine.

15. She loves _____ sky diving.

16. She's just graduated from university and is very excited about _____ future.

17. She works for _____ environment agency in Canada.

18. Did you see _____ moon last night? It was really bright.

19. They wished for _____ world peace.

20. He goes to _____ work on the train every day.

Part 7.2: Using *a/an* with uncountable nouns

An abstract noun is one which represents an idea (*beauty, love, peace*) rather than a real thing in the world. Nouns representing real objects in the world (*table, water, forest*) are called concrete nouns. Abstract nouns can be countable or uncountable.

We can sometimes choose to use *a/an* with abstract uncountable nouns. To use a word in this way, we must want to talk about a particular kind of the abstract noun. So instead of talking about 'anger' we must want to talk about a certain type of anger, for example 'a dreadful anger'. We usually show which kind of the noun we're talking about by putting an adjective in front of it, but we can also put a clause afterwards. This is usually only possible in formal or literary English.

Here are some examples:

anger	He felt **a** dreadful anger that he could not control.
calm	After the riots, **a** fragile calm descended on the city.
courage	I became aware of **a** courage that I didn't even know I had.
enthusiasm	She spoke with **a** great enthusiasm about the new plans.
evil	**A** terrible evil crossed the land.
friendship	**An** enduring friendship is a great comfort.
harm	**A** great harm was caused by his carelessness.
intelligence	That child has **a** rare intelligence.
joy	What **a** joy that baby is!
knowledge	He has **an** excellent knowledge of languages.
love	The couple shared **a** great love of dancing.
melancholy	**A** dreadful melancholy descended on the room.
patience	He showed **an** impressive patience with his toddler's demands.

peace	After the war, **an** uncertain peace gripped the region.
serenity	The gardens are pervaded by **a** calm serenity.
silence	When I walked in there was **an** awkward silence.
understanding	He showed **an** amazing understanding of the difficult material.
warmth	She welcomed us with **an** extraordinary warmth.

It's important to note that just because we're using *a/an* doesn't mean that the noun has become countable. For example, we still usually can't make a plural from these nouns ('They both felt dreadful angers').

A few of these phrases have become fixed expressions. They can be used in formal and informal English, and include:

- **a** good education
- **a** great help

On the other hand, there are some abstract nouns which never take *a/an*. This group includes:

advice	a fantastic advice	fantastic advice
fun	a really good fun	really good fun
health	an excellent health	excellent health
information	a useful information	useful information
luck	a terrible luck	terrible luck
news	a sad news	sad news
progress	an impressive progress	impressive progress
trouble	a deep trouble	deep trouble
weather (see also Part 4.11)*	a lovely weather	lovely weather
work (see also Part 7.4.3)	a hard work	hard work

* Although we can never say 'a + adjective + weather', it's possible to drop *the* when weather is modified. So we can say:

- The match was cancelled because of **the** weather [usual use of weather, with *the*].

- The match was cancelled because of Ø bad weather [bad weather that the listener doesn't know about].

- The match was cancelled because of **the** bad weather [bad weather that the listener does know about].

This use is not only for abstract nouns. We can also use *a/an* with some other uncountable nouns when we mean 'a certain kind of' (see also Appendix 2). For example:

- The beach was covered with **a** beautiful white sand.

- **A** gentle rain fell all night.

However, we can't use *a/an* with these concrete uncountable nouns:

furniture	~~a beautiful furniture~~	beautiful furniture
homework	~~a difficult homework~~	difficult homework
jewellery	~~an expensive jewellery~~	expensive jewellery
luggage	~~a practical luggage~~	practical luggage
money	~~a useful money~~	useful money

Also, (in a similar way to 'weather' above) countable nouns that usually take a certain article can sometimes change their article if they are used with an adjective that changes the meaning to 'a certain kind of':

| **the** sun | **a** bright red sun |
| **the** moon | **an** autumn moon |

Of course *sun* usually needs *the*, as we saw in Part 2.3. However, using 'a bright red sun' emphasises that this is a certain (perhaps unusual) aspect of the sun. Out of all the possible ways that the sun can look, this is one of them. You can also say 'the bright red sun', which is more neutral.

Note that the adjective usually has to go in front of the noun in all these cases:

- Did you have **an** interesting trip? [We both know which trip I mean, but I don't use *the* because I'm asking if, out of all possible trips, you had a certain kind of trip.]

but

- Was **the** trip interesting? [This is using 'trip' as a normal noun. I think the listener will know which trip I mean, so I use *the*. Then I ask something about that particular trip.]

Part 7.3: Institutions (*church, university, school* etc.)

The names of some institutions (such as *school* or *church*) have become part of fixed expressions. These fixed expressions use articles a little bit differently from normal.

When we think of certain institutions in general, especially when we think about them being used for their usual purpose (e.g. studying in university, being ill in hospital, praying in church), then we often use them with 'no article':

- I'm studying French at Ø university.
- My sister goes to Ø church every Sunday.

On the other hand, if we think about them just as buildings, rather than what they are used for, then we follow the normal rules for articles (as we do for other buildings since they are normal countable nouns):

- I'll meet you at **the** university [the listener knows which university building, so I use *the*].
- She works in a café near **a** hospital [the listener doesn't know which hospital building, so I use *a*].

Here is a more complete list:

church	• We used to go to Ø church every Sunday [intended purpose].
	• I'll meet you outside **the** church [thinking about a church as a building, so a normal noun – you know which church I mean].
class*	• Where's Julie? She's in Ø class [intended purpose].
	• John delivered the pizza to **the** class(room) [normal noun].

college	• She's at Ø college studying hairdressing [intended purpose]. • **The** college is next to the station [thinking of a college as a building, normal noun].
court	• He went to Ø court over his divorce [intended purpose]. • The children did a tour of **a** court [normal noun].
hospital	• Unfortunately, my neighbour is still in Ø hospital [intended purpose, he's ill]. • My mother went to **the** hospital to visit my aunt [normal noun, I'm thinking of a particular hospital that the listener knows, so I use *the*].
jail / prison	• His father is in Ø jail [intended purpose]. • Her new house is near **a** jail [normal noun].
school	• John's at Ø school at the moment [intended purpose]. • There's a party at **the** school on Friday night [normal noun].
university	• She's studying Spanish at Ø university [intended purpose]. • The comedian hates performing at Ø universities [normal noun; I use 'no article' because I'm talking about universities in general].

* Here, I'm talking about a physical classroom. The word *class* is also used to mean a certain group of students, in which case it's a normal noun.

EXERCISE 7.2

Fill the gap with *the* or no article (Ø).

1. The old actor died in _____ hospital last night.

2. She sometimes goes to _____ jail in our city as part of her job.

3. My son's studying history at _____ university.

4. When their houses were damaged in the storm, some people slept in _____ school nearby.

5. He spent three years in _____ prison.

6. Have you ever seen _____ university in Cambridge?

7. The lawyer stood up in _____ court and spoke to the jury.

8. _____ college in our city is very near the river.

9. Do your parents go to _____ church on Sundays?

10. Lucy is still at _____ school – she's only fourteen.

11. I won't break the law – I don't want to go to _____ jail!

12. My class visited _____ prison in our town last month – it was very interesting.

13. We'll meet outside _____ church at six.

14. The school children had a tour round _____ court near their school.

15. How many classes do you have at _____ college?

16. I went to _____ hospital today to see my friend who's a nurse.

Part 7.4: *Bed / home / work / town*

7.4.1 *Bed*

Bed is a strange word! If we don't use an article, it means a place where we sleep, not a particular object:

- The children are in Ø bed.
- We didn't get out of Ø bed until after one o'clock.
- She got home and went straight to Ø bed.

But when we are thinking about a bed as an object, we use articles in the normal way:

- She sat on **the** bed in my room [I choose *the* because the listener knows which bed I mean].
- I need to buy **a** new bed [I choose *a* because I don't know which bed yet, I'm not talking about a specific one].

7.4.2 *Home*

The word *home* is also a bit strange. We usually use 'no article':

- They went Ø home.*

- I stayed at Ø home.

- Julie works from Ø home.

- Lucy is at Ø home at the moment.

*Notice we don't need *to* with 'go home' (not 'go to home').

But we can use an article with *home* when it means 'the building that somebody lives (or used to live) in'. In this case we use articles in the normal way:

- We visited **the** home of Jackie Kennedy.

- My sister has made her flat into **a** beautiful home.

[It's also possible to use 'home' as short for 'retirement home' or similar expression. We use articles in the normal way:

- Her grandmother is too frail to stay in her own house, so she lives in a (retirement) home.]

7.4.3 *Work* (used as a noun)

When we think about *work* as a place, then we don't need to use an article with it:

- She's at Ø work.

- I arrive at Ø work at nine.

- We leave Ø work every day at six.

- You should go to Ø work earlier.

We usually don't use *a/an* with *work*. We can sometimes use *the* if we are talking about some specific work that the listener knows about.

- **The** work I'm doing at the moment is very interesting.

[An exception is when *work* means w*ork of art/literature/music*. In this case *work* is a normal countable noun.]

7.4.4 *Town*

When we are thinking about the town centre near to us, we often use 'no article' with certain expressions:

- *In town* — John's in town at the moment.
- *Go into town* — Shall we go into town this afternoon?
- *Leave town* — He left town after he argued with his wife.

Of course, *town* can also be a normal noun:

- **The** town where I live is quite small [we use *the* because the listener knows which one].

EXERCISE 7.3

Fill the gap with *the* or no article (Ø).

1. John is at _____ home now.

2. Let's go into _____ town later – I'd like to do some shopping.

3. I went to _____ bed early last night, but I still feel tired.

4. _____ work that Julie is doing at the moment sounds boring.

5. My son's just rented his first flat and needs furniture – I'm going to give him _____ bed in our spare room.

6. I usually arrive at _____ work at about eight thirty.

7. She bought a book about _____ homes of the rich and famous.

8. _____ town where my mother lives is very pretty.

Part 7.5: Illnesses

There are a few common illnesses which we often use with *the*:*

- *the flu* — John has the flu.
- *the measles* — I had the measles when I was two.
- *the hiccups* — Do you know a way to stop the hiccups?

*It is also possible to use 'no article', with no change in meaning.

Many illnesses are normal uncountable nouns (for example, *cancer* and *heart disease*). As we saw in Section 3, we use 'no article' to talk about these in general:

- Ø Cancer is unfortunately a big problem.
- A lot of people suffer from Ø heart disease.

Other illnesses are normal countable nouns:

- She caught **a** cold (I don't know which cold so we use *a*).
- He's had three colds this winter.
- **The** cold that I caught last month was really horrible (we know which cold because of the relative clause so we use *the*).

The same is true of *cough, chill, fever, temperature* and *headache*:

- I often get **a** cough.
- She caught **a** chill when she was camping.
- My son has **a** fever.
- She was vomiting and had **a** temperature.
- I have **a** headache.

EXERCISE 7.4

Fill the gap with *the* if possible. If not, use 'no article' (Ø) or *a/an*.

1. She has never had _____ measles.

2. Unfortunately, he was diagnosed with _____ cancer.

3. I felt ill, but I didn't have _____ temperature.

4. Her grandfather suffered from _____ heart disease.

5. Julie has _____ cold, so she's not coming swimming today.

6. John had _____ fever, and felt terrible.

7. He had _____ flu during the Christmas holidays.

8. I have such _____ headache. I think I'll go to bed early.

9. She had _____ cough all winter.

10. I very often get _____ hiccups.

Part 7.6: Acronyms and initialisms

Sometimes, we use the first letter (or first part) of each word in a long name to make a shorter version. So instead of saying 'British Broadcasting Corporation' we say 'BBC', and instead of saying 'North Atlantic Treaty Organisation', we say 'NATO'. An initialism is when each letter of the abbreviation is pronounced. An example is *BBC*. We say 'B-B-C', using the names of the letters. On the other hand, an acronym is when we pronounce the letters as if they were a word, and we don't use the names of the letters. For example, we say 'NATO' all together as a word.

7.6.1 Initialisms

Common nouns (these behave like normal common nouns):

AC (air conditioning) (uncountable)	Please turn on the AC [I use *the* because we know which AC I mean].
ATM (automated teller machine) (countable)	I've run out of cash, so I need to find an ATM.
B&B (bed and breakfast) (countable)	They went to Wales for the weekend and stayed in a B&B.
DNA (deoxyribonucleic acid) (uncountable)	Both his parents are tall, so he will be tall too. It's in his DNA.
ID (identification) (uncountable)	In the UK you need ID to buy alcohol if you look young.
IQ (intelligence quotient) (countable)	He has a very high IQ.
ISBN (International Standard Book Number) (countable)	Does his book have an ISBN?
PR (public relations) (uncountable)	She got a job in PR.
SPF (sun protection factor) (countable)	What SPF is this sun cream?

| UFO (unidentified flying object) (countable) | She claims she saw a UFO in the sky last night. |

Proper nouns (these often have *the*):

The BBC (British Broadcasting Corporation)	I watched a very interesting programme on **the** BBC last night. [But note: 'I watched a programme on Ø BBC2 last night.' See Part 6.3.]
The CIA (Central Intelligence Agency)	He was followed by **the** CIA.
The EU (European Union)	Since Italy is part of **the** EU, a British person doesn't need a visa to go there.
The FBI (Federal Bureau of Investigation)	I watched a film about **the** FBI.
The NBA (National Basketball Association)	He used to play in **the** NBA.
The UN (United Nations)	She works for **the** UN.
The WHO (World Health Organization)	**The** WHO recommends that all children are immunised.

But be careful. Not all proper nouns follow this pattern:

CNN (Cable News Network)	When I was abroad, the only English channel I had was Ø CNN.
TfL (Transport for London)	Ø TfL manages more than 700 bus routes in London.

See Appendix 1 for information about pronouncing the names of letters.

7.6.2 Acronyms

Common nouns (these behave like normal common nouns):

FAQ (frequently asked questions) (countable)	Have a look at the FAQ on the website and see if the answer to your question is there.
PIN (personal identification number) (countable)	Never write down a PIN! You need to memorise it.

'A' AND 'THE' EXPLAINED • 95

RAM (random access memory) (uncountable)	How much RAM does your computer have?

Proper nouns (these usually have 'no article'):

NASA (National Aeronautical and Space Administration)	He worked for Ø NASA for twenty years.
NATO (North Atlantic Treaty Organization)	Ø NATO has its headquarters in Belgium.
OPEC (Organization of Petroleum Exporting Countries)	Which countries are members of Ø OPEC?
UNICEF (United Nations Children's Fund)	She donated some money to Ø UNICEF.

If we use the expanded versions of these, they often need *the*. However, we almost always use the acronym.

EXERCISE 7.5

Fill the gap with the correct article.

1. I don't like _____ AC at work. It's too cold.

2. Should we book _____ B&B or a hotel for our holiday?

3. She's studying _____ DNA at university.

4. Where is the headquarters of _____ NASA?

5. Do you know _____ ISBN of the book you want?

6. You should use a sun cream with _____ high SPF if you have fair skin.

7. There are a lot of stories about _____ UFOs. People find the idea of life on other planets interesting.

8. She's wanted to work for _____ BBC for a long time.

9. In the film, the hero is running away from _____ CIA.

10. Is there _____ ATM outside the station?

11. How many member states are there in _____ EU?

12. He worked as a reporter for _____ CNN.

13. The headquarters of _____ FBI is in Washington D.C.

14. There are thirty basketball clubs in _____ NBA.

15. He left _____ UNICEF some money in his will.

16. _____ UN sent aid to the country after the earthquake.

17. When does _____ WHO recommend weaning babies?

18. The website has _____ FAQ, but I couldn't find the information that I wanted there.

19. I need to call the bank and ask them to send me _____ new PIN.

20. Lord Ismay was the first Secretary General of _____ NATO.

Part 7.7: *A little*, and *little*, *a few* and *few*

We use *a/an* with several quantifiers:

- a little
- a few
- a lot (of).

We also use 'no article' with several:

- little
- few
- lots (of).

In many situations, we can choose to use *a little* or *little* (when using an uncountable noun), or *a few* or *few* (when using a plural countable noun). They have slightly different meanings.

When we say *a little* or *a few* we mean a small amount, but it's enough:

- JOHN: Let's go out tonight. LUCY: Okay. I have **a little** money, enough for the cinema at least.

On the other hand, *little* or *few* usually give us a different impression. These also mean a small amount, but this time the amount is almost nothing. If the noun denotes something that we want (like money or friends) then using *little* or *few* means that we don't have enough:

- JOHN: Let's go out tonight. LUCY: Sorry, I have **little** money. I really can't afford to go out.

Of course, if we use *few* or *little* with something we don't want, then the sentence can have a positive meaning. It's good to have nearly no problems, for example:

- There have been **few** problems with the new system, thankfully!
- Luckily, there is **little** crime in my town.
- I'm so pleased that I have **few** arguments with my family.
- It's great that there's been very **little** bad weather this month.

A lot and *lots* aren't like this. *A lot* means the same as *lots*.

EXERCISE 7.6

Choose *a little / little / a few / few*.

1. I have _____ water left. There's enough to share.

2. I have _____ good friends. I'm not lonely.

3. He has _____ education. He can't read or write, and he can hardly count.

4. There are _____ people she really trusts. It's a bit sad.

5. We've got _____ time at the weekend. Would you like to meet?

6. Julie gave us _____ apples from her garden. Shall we share them?

7. She has _____ self-confidence. She has a lot of trouble talking to new people.

8. There are _____ women politicians in the UK. There should be more.

9. It's a great pity, but this hospital has _____ medicine. They can't help many people.

10. I've got _____ cakes to give away. Would you like one?

11. There's _____ milk left in the fridge. It should be enough for our coffee.

12. _____ children from this school go on to university, unfortunately.

13. Do you need information on English grammar? I have _____ books on the topic if you would like to borrow them.

14. She's lucky. She has _____ problems.

15. The UK has _____ sunshine in the winter. That's why so many British people go on holiday to sunny places!

16. There's _____ spaghetti left in the cupboard. Shall we eat it tonight?

17. There are _____ programmes on television that I want to watch. I prefer to download a film or read a book.

18. He has _____ free time. He hardly ever even manages to call his mother!

19. Unfortunately, I have _____ problems at the moment.

20. Are you thirsty? There's _____ juice left in this bottle, if you'd like it.

Part 7.8: *Most* and *the most*

Most can be used before a noun to mean 'almost all' or 'very many'. In this case, we don't use *the*:

- Ø Most people like chocolate.
- Ø Most cats catch mice.
- Ø Most children drink milk.

We can also use *most of the* + noun with the same meaning, if the noun is specific:

- Ø Most of the people in the class like cake.
- Ø Most of the cats in London wear collars.
- Ø Most of the children that I know drink apple juice.

The most is part of the superlative when we use a long adjective. It gives us the idea of a comparison (see Part 2.4.5 for more about superlatives):

- Lucy is **the** most intelligent student in the class.

The most can also be followed by a noun, but there has to be a comparison implied. In this case, *most books* = 'the largest number of books':

- James has **the** most books of the people in the class.

EXERCISE 7.7

Fill the gap with *most* or *the most*.

1. She's _____ beautiful girl that I've ever seen.

2. _____ British people eat turkey at Christmas.

3. _____ of the clothes in that shop are badly made.

4. I think that _____ intelligent thing to do is to take a taxi.

5. He's _____ interesting person I've spoken to today.

6. I think that _____ students will be very happy that the exams are finished.

7. _____ of the cars on my street are black.

8. That is _____ delicious cake that I've ever eaten!

9. The teacher told me that _____ of the children in her class like science.

10. I love living in London. I think it's _____ exciting city in the world!

Part 7.9: *A/an* or *one*?

7.9.1 Choosing *a/an* or *one*

We often use *a/an* instead of *one*. This is very common before the numbers *hundred*, *thousand* and *million*, as well as fractions like *third* and *quarter*:

- My great-aunt is **a** hundred years old.

- It cost **a** thousand pounds.

- The library has over **a** million books.

- About **a** quarter of the earth's surface is covered by land.

We can usually use either *a/an* or *one*. If we use *one*, it emphasises the number – that it's one thing, and only one thing. *A/an* is more neutral, and much more normal in English.

- ME: I'd like **a** cup of coffee, please.

WAITRESS: Two coffees?

ME: No, **one** cup of coffee.

Another situation where we use *one* and not *a/an* is when we are talking about one of a group or a larger number, with the phrases *of the...*, *of these...* or *of those...*

- One of the students cheated in the exam [not 'An of the students cheated in the exam'].
- I think Madonna lives in one of these houses [not 'an of these houses'].

EXERCISE 7.8

Choose *a/an* or *one* (whichever is more natural).

1. Have you only got _____ brother? Jessie said you had three.

2. Only _____ of the students in my class passed the exam.

3. Could I have _____ cup of tea please.

4. I'd like _____ beer, not two.

5. There are at least _____ million people living in that city.

6. She's got _____ cat and _____ dog.

7. _____ of my friends was late but all the others were on time.

8. I'd like _____ large sandwich.

9. Julie's got _____ car, not seven!

10. There was _____ motorbike on the corner of the street.

11. Please give me _____ piece of paper.

12. He has _____ hundred pounds in his wallet.

13. He paid more than _____ thousand pounds for the ring.

14. He bought _____ of the TVs we looked at last week.

15. Can I have _____ of those doughnuts?

16. Can I have _____ glass of water?

17. Sorry, I only wanted _____ cup of coffee, not three!

18. She bought _____ car last week.

19. _____ of my friends lives in Shanghai.

20. _____ of these days I must clean out my garage.

7.9.2 *A/an* and *one* with *half*

With the word 'half' (although it's a fraction) we don't usually use *one*. Instead, we generally use 'no article'.

- Could I have Ø half of the pizza, please?
- She gave us Ø half of the flowers.
- It's Ø half past four.
- We walked along the beach for about Ø half an hour.

However, if we use *half* after a number, then we usually use *a*.

- It took **two and a half** hours to get to the airport.
- I worked at that school for **six and a half** years.
- My son is **three and a half**.
- I bought **one and a half** metres of fabric.

We also use *a* with *half* when it's used after a word that tells us how much or how long. The time word or the amount word must also be used with *a* (not with *one*).

- We were in Paris for **a week** and **a half**. [We can't say 'We were in Paris for one week and a half'. But it's fine to say 'We were in Paris for one and a half weeks'].
- He ate **a slice** and **a half** of cake. [Not 'He ate one slice and a half of cake'. But it's fine to say 'He ate one and a half slices of cake'].

With other numbers we must put the words *a half* after the number, not after the time or amount word:

- We travelled for **five and a half months**. [Not 'We travelled for five months and a half'].
- I bought **six and a half litres** of water. [Not 'I bought six litres and a half of water'].

EXERCISE 7.9

Choose *a/an* or *one*:

1. She's lived here for _____ year and a half.

2. She's lived here for _____ and a half years.

3. I bought _____ and a half kilos of tomatoes.

4. I bought _____ kilo and a half of tomatoes.

5. He was away for _____ week and a half.

6. He was away for _____ and a half weeks.

7. Luke walked _____ mile and a half to the party.

8. Luke walked _____ and a half miles to the party.

9. They arrived here _____ and a half months ago.

10. They arrived here _____ month and a half ago.

With clock times, we usually use 'no article' with *half*:

- It's Ø half past three [= it's 3:30].
- The class starts at Ø half past eight.

With 'quarter past' and 'quarter to' we can use 'no article' or *a* with no change in meaning.

- It's **(a)** quarter past four [= 4:15].
- Let's meet at **(a)** quarter to seven [= 6:45].

Part 7.10: Using *a/an* instead of *per*

We can use *a/an* when we are talking about 'how much' or 'how often', instead of *per*. *Per* sounds a bit more formal, while *a/an* is more normal.

How much:

- The train goes at 200 kilometres **an** hour
- She studies for three hours **a** day.

- The tomatoes are $3 **a** kilo.
- The eggs are £2 **a** box.

How often:

- She goes to the gym three times **a** week.
- He brushes his teeth twice **a** day.
- I visit my grandparents several times **a** year.
- We go to the cinema twice **a** month.

However, we don't need to use an article if we have *every* or *each*:

- I call my mother every Ø day [but 'I call my mother once **a** day'].

EXERCISE 7.10

Choose *a/an* or 'no article' (Ø).

1. I play football twice _____ week.

2. She calls her parents every _____ Sunday.

3. She's driving at 50 miles _____ hour.

4. The new train will go at 300 kilometres _____ hour.

5. The bananas cost £2 _____ kilo.

6. I meet my friend Julie every _____ week.

7. The water is 50 cents _____ litre.

8. We go out for dinner twice _____ month.

9. She goes to the gym three times _____ week.

10. I go on holiday to Spain every _____ year.

11. I work at the school a few days _____ month.

12. The ribbon cost £1 _____ metre.

13. He runs ten kilometres _____ day.

14. John has a meeting with his boss every _____ week.

15. The speed limit in London is 30 miles _____ hour.

16. Petrol is £1.50 _____ litre.

17. Lisa calls her grandfather twice _____ week.

18. I go to the library every _____ Saturday.

19. Those sandals are £10 _____ pair.

20. I visit my family every _____ year.

Part 7.11: *Next* and *last* with time expressions

In Part 2.4.4, we saw that we often use *the* with the adjectives *next* and *last*. However, when we use *next* and *last* with time expressions they usually don't take *the*. For example, when *next week* means 'the week after this one' we don't need *the*:

- I'm going to visit my brother Ø next week [not '~~the next week~~'].

Similarly, when *last week* means 'the week before this one', we don't need *the*:

- I saw David Ø last week [not '~~the last week~~'].

This applies for similar expressions such as *next month, next year, last month, last year, last night, last summer, next winter*. It's also true with days of the week, like *next Tuesday, last Sunday*:

- I saw the new James Bond film Ø last month.
- We're going on holiday Ø next month.
- She will graduate Ø next year.
- I went on holiday to Bolivia Ø last summer.

EXERCISE 7.11

Choose *the* or 'no article' (Ø).

1. I'm meeting Julie _____ next week.

2. We'll get on _____ next bus.

3. I arrived in New York _____ last month.

4. I can't believe he ate _____ last chocolate!

5. I'm going on holiday _____ next Friday.

6. She started college _____ last year.

7. I liked _____ last teacher. I don't think the new one is as good.

8. What are you doing _____ next month?

9. She asked directions from _____ next person she saw.

10. We didn't see John at all _____ last week.

11. Call me _____ next Tuesday.

12. I visited Kenya _____ last winter.

Two more points:

1. With *last time / next time* we can use either *the* or 'no article':

- **The / Ø** next time we go out, I'll bring my umbrella.

- **The / Ø** last time I saw her, she looked really tired.

2. When we use *in* with *next*, or *last* as in 'in the next year', we use *the*, and the phrase has a different meaning. *Next year* = 'the year after this one':

- I'm going to Russia **Ø next year**.

But *in the next year* = 'between now and one year from now':

- I'll finish my thesis **in the next year**. [If today is the 1st of June 2014, I will finish some time between now and the 1st of June 2015.]

In the same way *last week* = 'the week before this one':

- We met **Ø last week**.

But *in the last week* = 'between one week ago and now':

- I lost my credit card sometime **in the last week**, but I'm not sure when. [If today is Tuesday, I lost my card sometime between last Tuesday and now].

Part 7.12: *First / second / third*

We often use *the* with ordinal numbers such as *first, second, third* and so on, if they make it clear to the listener which one we mean:

- She bought **the** first dress she found.

- Which book do you want?' '**The** second one.'

- I'd like **the** third cake on the shelf.

Again, it's also possible to use *a/an* with these numbers, if they don't tell the listener exactly which one we mean, although this is much less common:

- Would you like **a** second cup of coffee?

This really means 'would you like one more cup of coffee?'. It doesn't mean 'would you like the second cup of coffee in a row of cups of coffee?'. Other examples include:

- The band released **a** first album in 2010 and **a** second in 2012.

- We missed two buses, but thankfully **a** third bus came along and we got on.

Exception: we often use 'no article' with *first [second, third...] prize* and *first [second, third...] place* when talking about races or competitions. This is a fixed expression (see Section 8 for more about idioms and fixed expressions).

Also, we don't use *the* when we are using these words alone to put ideas in order. For example:

- **First**, you mix the flour, salt and yeast. **Second**, you add the water. **Third**, you knead the dough for about ten minutes.

EXERCISE 7.12

If it's possible, put 'no article' (Ø). If not, put *the*.

1. Lucy came in _____ first place in the riding competition.

2. I won _____ second prize! Hurray!

3. Why don't I like living here? _____ first, it's too cold. Also, I miss my family.

4. I'd like _____ third cake on the shelf, please.

5. John went to the bank _____ first. Then he went to the library.

6. 'Which bottle do you want?' '_____ second one.'

7. She got on _____ first bus that came.

8. I've read _____ first book in the series, but I haven't read _____ second one.

9. 'How did Luke do in the race?' 'He came _____ third.'

10. Could you pass me _____ second cup on the right, please?

Part 7.13: *The* with comparatives

Finally, we have a completely different use of *the*, with certain comparative structures. We can use '*the* + comparative ... *the* + comparative' to say that two adjectives change together:

- **The** sunnier it is, **the** happier I am. [As it becomes sunnier, so I become happier. The two things are linked.]

Here are some more examples:

- **The** better the student, **the** higher the grade.
- **The** sweeter the cake, **the** more delicious it is.
- **The** bigger the car, **the** more annoying the driver!

We can also use *more* + noun in this structure:

- **The** more work you do, **the** better your result will be.
- **The** more friends I have, **the** happier I feel.

We also often use *the better* alone in the second half of this kind of expression:

- **The** hotter the curry, **the** better!

Section 7 Review Exercises

EXERCISE 7.13

Choose the correct article.

1. I stayed in bed for a week when I had _____ flu.

2. I'll see you _____ next Tuesday.

3. I've got such _____ headache! Do you have any painkillers?

4. Fortunately, not many children get _____ measles nowadays.

5. She sees her family once _____ month.

6. _____ more it rains in London, _____ more I want a holiday!

7. There are _____ few biscuits left – would you like one?

8. She goes to the gym three times _____ week.

9. He usually watches the news on _____ BBC.

10. Could I just have _____ half a cup of coffee, please.

11. She donates money to _____ UNICEF every month

12. Jenny is _____ most intelligent student in the class.

13. John is at _____ hospital where he's visiting a friend.

14. The thief was sent to _____ jail for six years.

15. When I was at _____ university, none of the students had any money.

16. She gave _____ million pounds to charity.

17. Meet me _____ next week.

18. She arrives in New York _____ next month.

19. She has _____ few nice clothes, so she always looks scruffy.

20. I go to the cinema about twice _____ month.

EXERCISE 7.14

Choose the correct article.

1. He has at least _____ hundred DVDs.

2. _____ more chocolate I eat, _____ happier I am!

3. He brushes his teeth twice _____ day.

4. I have _____ little money, so let's buy some ice cream.

5. She earns _____ thousand pounds a month.

6. We visited Canada _____ last year.

7. I went to _____ bed at nine o'clock last night.

8. He saw a photographer standing outside _____ court.

9. John used to work as a cleaner at _____ college.

10. _____ faster the car, _____ more he likes it.

11. The school children enjoyed going to _____ old jail.

12. They went to _____ court during their divorce proceedings.

13. I think _____ most people would like to have a bit more free time.

14. We meet twice or three times _____ year.

15. She has _____ little money, so she can't afford to heat her flat.

16. John's at _____ work at the moment.

17. She came to San Francisco _____ last December.

18. She's had _____ cold for three weeks.

19. Her grandfather had _____ heart disease.

20. Lucy's still at _____ school – she's studying for her exams at the moment.

EXERCISE 7.15

Choose the correct article.

1. My grandmother goes to _____ church every week.

2. _____ church in my village is to be knocked down.

3. My hotel room didn't have _____ AC.

4. Could you pass me _____ third book on the right, please?

5. What's _____ most terrifying movie you've ever seen?

6. _____ most animals in the UK are harmless.

7. She applied for a job at _____ university.

8. We went to _____ school to vote in the general election.

9. What are you studying at _____ college?

10. John had _____ temperature, so he went home.

11. She stayed in _____ hospital for a few days after she had her baby.

12. Let's go _____ home. I'm tired.

13. I need _____ new PIN.

14. I'd like to go into _____ town later. There are some things I'd like to buy.

15. I've recently started taking _____ piano lessons.

16. She bought _____ ballet shoes.

17. She works in _____ internet café.

18. Is there _____ football pitch near here?

19. _____ stronger the coffee, _____ better!

20. Emily won _____ first prize in the competition.

(Remember that you can download all the exercises as printable PDFs at www.perfect-english-grammar.com/a-and-the.html.)

Section 8: Idioms And Fixed Expressions

In English there are lots of 'fixed expressions'. These are groups of words that always go together. Often, there is a historical reason for them, but, sorry, they're not logical! We have to learn each one, like a single piece of vocabulary.

Part 8.1: Prepositional phrases

Here are some examples of prepositional phrases, a type of fixed expression.

a/an	the	no article
at **a** disadvantage	in **the** habit of	by **Ø** mistake
at **a** glance	behind **the** scenes	in **Ø** brief
at **a** loose end	for **the** sake of	in **Ø** danger
at **a** profit	in **the** distance	in **Ø** front of
for **a** change	in **the** long run	in **Ø** general
for **a** good cause	in **the** meantime	in **Ø** half
in **a** hurry	in **the** way	in **Ø** love
in **a** sense	on **the** contrary	in **Ø** particular
on **a** diet	on **the** increase	in **Ø** secret
on **a** regular basis	on **the** off-chance	in **Ø** touch
to **a** certain extent	on **the** other hand	on **Ø** purpose
with **a** view to	on **the** whole	on **Ø** tiptoe

EXERCISE 8.1

Fill the gap with the correct article.

1. She bought some jewellery abroad, and sold it at _____ profit when she got home.

2. John's solution is correct to _____ certain extent. It will help, but it won't fix the problem completely.

3. I could see a mountain range in _____ distance.

4. I really like the museums in London, but I like the British Museum in _____ particular.

5. I love living in London on _____ whole (very occasionally it's difficult).

6. He seems nice normally, but behind _____ scenes he makes some deals I don't approve of.

7. He didn't realise he was in _____ danger from the tide until the coastguard arrived.

8. My brother was at _____ loose end at home, so he was pleased when his friend called.

9. Crime is on _____ increase. You should be careful of your bag.

10. I didn't break the vase on _____ purpose, Mummy! It was an accident.

11. David could tell at _____ glance that the news was bad.

12. I wanted to get some plums but I bought peaches by _____ mistake.

13. I called Julie on _____ off-chance that she was free for lunch.

14. That radio station reports the news in _____ brief at 7 a.m.

15. Our shower will be fixed next week. In _____ meantime, we can use the shower at the gym.

16. She thought she'd get better results if she studied harder, but, on _____ contrary, she needed to relax more instead.

17. I bought an old car with _____ view to fixing it up.

18. She crossed the room on _____ tiptoe, as the baby had just fallen asleep.

19. Julie is on _____ diet again! She's always trying to lose weight.

20. Are you in _____ habit of studying every day? If not, you need to start!

21. I made him a birthday cake in _____ secret.

22. The charity ball was for _____ good cause, so many people gave money.

23. I was in _____ hurry this morning and I forgot my umbrella.

24. Your wallet is in _____ front of the TV.

25. She likes her job in _____ general, but this week has been very stressful.

26. Please cut that piece of cake in _____ half. It's too much for one person!

27. Unfortunately, I don't see my old friends on _____ regular basis. We only meet rarely.

28. The doctor told him to stop smoking for _____ sake of his health.

29. In _____ sense, Rebecca is right. What she says is partly true.

30. I couldn't get to the door quickly because my suitcase was in _____ way.

31. If you don't get private tuition for the exam, you are at _____ disadvantage.

32. I usually drink tea, but today I thought I'd have coffee for _____ change.

33. It's difficult to study every day, but in _____ long run it will be worth it.

34. John loves living in the countryside. I, on _____ other hand, prefer the city.

35. I'm still in _____ touch with friends from school. We meet once a year.

36. Richard has been behaving very strangely recently. Perhaps he's in _____ love!

Part 8.2: Idioms

Idioms sometimes follow the normal rules about *a/an* and *the* but sometimes they don't. The best idea is to learn idioms as a single piece of vocabulary, by learning them whole, instead of learning each word. Here are some examples of English idioms.

no article	
as easy as Ø pie	= very easy
cry over Ø spilt milk	= be upset about something that you can't change now
make Ø ends meet	= have enough money for everyday things
see Ø eye to Ø eye	= agree (with someone)

| when Ø pigs fly | = probably never |

a/an	
call it **a** day	= finish what you're doing
give someone **a** hand	= help someone
make **a** mountain out of **a** molehill	= be too worried about something small
no room to swing **a** cat	= very small (of a house or room)
turn **a** blind eye	= pretend you don't see something

the	
beat about **the** bush	= avoid saying directly what you mean
kick **the** bucket	= die
out of **the** blue	= very unexpectedly
tie **the** knot	= get married
under **the** weather	= a bit ill

EXERCISE 8.2

Fill the gap with the correct article.

1. This exercise is as easy as _____ pie.

2. My flat is absolutely tiny – there's no room to swing _____ cat.

3. It's no use crying over _____ spilt milk – the money is all gone.

4. I don't think Julie will come to the party tonight – she's feeling a bit under _____ weather.

5. It's difficult for them to make _____ ends meet.

6. Don't beat about _____ bush – say exactly what you think.

7. He often turned _____ blind eye to his employee's lateness, but today she went too far.

8. If his grandfather kicks _____ bucket, he'll be in trouble.

9. Let's call it _____ day. I'm tired and I'd like to go home.

10. My sister and I don't really see eye to _____ eye. We disagree on almost everything.

11. I got a letter from an old school friend out of _____ blue.

12. Don't make _____ mountain out of _____ molehill. The situation isn't as bad as you think.

13. They got engaged last week and plan to tie _____ knot next year.

14. She'll see him again when _____ pigs fly!

15. Please give me _____ hand with my homework. I don't know how to begin it.

Part 8.3: Parallel structures

Parallel structures are a kind of fixed expression where either a word is repeated (e.g. *arm in arm*) or two closely linked words are used (e.g. *from north to south*). These often take 'no article' even when the nouns are singular, countable nouns:

- They walked Ø arm in Ø arm along the riverbank.
- My English is improving Ø day by Ø day.
- We need to meet Ø face to Ø face. It's too hard to talk on the phone.
- They covered the country from Ø north to Ø south.
- He worked from Ø dawn to Ø dusk for years.

It's also possible to use 'no article' in some other, similar cases. These are not really fixed phrases, as we can change some things, but the nouns involved tend to be closely connected in meaning, and are often used with *and*, *both ...... and,* or *neither ... nor*. This use of 'no article' has a literary feel:

- The relationship between Ø mother and Ø child is an intense one.
- Neither Ø husband nor Ø wife knew the truth.
- Ø Knife, Ø fork and Ø spoon clattered to the ground.
- He held the letter between Ø finger and Ø thumb.

- The plague swept over Ø field and Ø forest.
- Exercise benefits both Ø mind and Ø body.

Section 8 Review Exercises

EXERCISE 8.3

Choose the correct article.

1. You're always at _____ loose end! Why don't you do something useful?

2. I think we should call it _____ day. I'm exhausted.

3. Even though I was in the middle of the city, I could see hills in _____ distance.

4. In _____ brief, what would you say the main problems are?

5. I try to save a little money every week. It'll be very useful in _____ long run.

6. I really hate mice and I hate mice in my house in _____ particular.

7. We usually go on holiday to Scotland, but this year we visited Paris for _____ change.

8. They only tied _____ knot last July, but they are already arguing.

9. Do you have meetings with your manager on _____ regular basis, or just now and then?

10. Obesity is on _____ increase, despite the best efforts of the government.

11. Learning English is as easy as _____ pie! No problem!

12. The young man met his girlfriend in _____ secret.

13. I don't always see _____ eye to eye with my boss, but he's okay.

14. The teacher turned _____ blind eye to his students leaving early on Friday afternoon. It was a lovely sunny day.

15. Dinner will be ready in an hour, but in _____ meantime, let's have some bread.

16. I felt at _____ disadvantage in the lecture, because all the other students had studied the material before.

17. I was feeling a bit under _____ weather, so I decided to go to bed early.

18. The little boy told his mother that he hadn't dropped the milk bottle on _____ purpose.

19. Could you please move your bicycle? It's in _____ way.

20. I couldn't reach the shelf, even on _____ tiptoe, so I had to get a ladder.

(Remember that you can download all the exercises as printable PDFs at www.perfect-english-grammar.com/a-and-the.html.)

Section 9: Proper Nouns

Part 9.1: Hints about proper nouns

Here are some tips about using articles with proper nouns. (See Appendix 2 for an explanation of the difference between common nouns and proper nouns.)

- Plural proper nouns usually take *the* (**the** Netherland**s**, **the** United State**s**).

- Proper noun phrases that include *of* usually take *the* (**the** University **of** Cambridge).

- Proper nouns that include an adjective often take *the* (**the Open** University).

- Proper nouns that include a possessive usually have 'no article' (Ø St Martin**'s** Theatre).

Part 9.2: Geographical names

9.2.1 'No article'

Place	Example	Exceptions / Notes
Lakes	We visited Ø Lake Geneva.	
Mountains	I saw Ø Mount Fuji from the aeroplane.	**The** Matterhorn.
Continents	She loves living in Ø Asia.	The continent Ø Antarctica has 'no article' but the regions '**the** Antarctic' and '**the** Arctic' take *the*.
Most countries	She travelled to Ø Chile last year.	The USA / the United States, the Netherlands, the Philippines, the United Kingdom / the UK.

Counties, states, provinces, regions	They live in Ø New Jersey. She loves Ø Provence.	Regions ending in 'north', 'south', 'east', 'west' (**the** Middle East), plurals (**the** Cotswolds, **the** Tropics).
Cities, towns, villages	He stayed in Ø Paris for a week last year.	**The** Hague [note that 'the' is part of the name and so *The Hague* always has a capital letter].
Islands	Ø Bali is popular with Australian tourists.	
Bays	We visited Ø San Francisco Bay.	Bays with of (the Bay of Bengal).

EXERCISE 9.1: COUNTRIES

Fill the gap with *the* or 'no article' (Ø).

1. She travelled around _____ India last year.

2. I've never met anyone from _____ Chile.

3. We went on holiday to _____ Philippines.

4. Julie lived in _____ Japan for a year.

5. I wish we could visit _____ Spain.

6. _____ Turkey has some beautiful cities.

7. London is in _____ United Kingdom.

8. Did you visit _____ Mexico on your trip?

9. I'd love to go to _____ United States.

10. Have you ever been to _____ Colombia?

11. She comes from _____ UK.

12. I met a girl from _____ Mongolia last night.

13. How many times has John been to _____ China?

14. Last year he visited _____ New Zealand.

15. San Francisco is in _____ USA.

16. My brother lives in _____ Morocco.

17. I saw a television programme about _____ South Korea.

18. She went on holiday to _____ Russia.

19. I've never been to _____ Mexico.

20. Jan comes from _____ Netherlands.

9.2.2 *The*

Place	Example
Rivers	**The** river Nile flows through Egypt.
	The Severn is the longest river in the UK.
Mountain ranges	We ski in **the** Alps every year.
Deserts	She travelled across **the** Sahara.
Oceans and seas (and parts of seas, like the Gulf of Mexico; not bays)	We sailed around **the** Mediterranean.
Groups of islands	They went to **the** Canary Islands.
Lines and points on the earth	They crossed **the** Tropic of Capricorn, **the** Equator, **the** Arctic Circle and **the** International Date Line.
	They hiked to **the** North Pole.

EXERCISE 9.2: LAKES, DESERTS, OCEANS, RIVERS

Fill the gap with the or 'no article' (Ø).

1. She has never been to _____ Lake Geneva.

2. They crossed _____ Sahara Desert by camel.

3. He flew across _____ Atlantic Ocean.

4. I've heard _____ Mekong is a very large river.

5. _____ Great Victoria Desert is in Australia.

6. Where is _____ Lake Titicaca?

7. Hawaii is in _____ Pacific Ocean.

8. He owns a house near _____ Lake Superior.

9. She lives near _____ river Thames.

10. We sailed around _____ Mediterranean.

11. _____ Kalahari Desert is in the south of Africa.

12. I'd love to visit _____ Red Sea.

13. _____ Lake Victoria is the largest lake in Africa.

14. Have you been to _____ Gobi Desert?

15. Her city is near _____ Yangtze River.

16. They went to an island in _____ Indian Ocean.

17. They went down _____ Amazon in a canoe.

18. People say that there is a monster in the bottom of _____ Loch Ness.

19. Is _____ Mississippi the longest river in the USA?

20. _____ Arabian Desert reaches from Egypt to Iran.

EXERCISE 9.3: MOUNTAINS, MOUNTAIN RANGES, REGIONS, CITIES

Fill the gap with the or 'no article'(Ø).

1. Have you ever seen _____ Mount Fuji?

2. Brandon is from _____ California.

3. _____ Mount Cook is very beautiful.

4. He loves going to _____ Pyrenees.

5. Where did you stay in _____ Delhi?

6. My parents live in _____ New Jersey.

7. What's your favourite part of _____ London?

8. I've heard _____ Himalayas are very beautiful.

9. She lived in _____ New York for three years.

10. She visited _____ Andes.

11. He grew up near _____ Rocky Mountains in the USA.

12. She has a house in _____ Sussex.

13. Sydney is in _____ New South Wales.

14. Where is _____ Mount Ararat?

15. I've always wanted to visit _____ Tuscany.

16. We went to _____ Paris last July.

17. We went skiing in _____ Alps.

18. He had decided to climb _____ Everest.

19. _____ Mont Blanc is the highest mountain in Europe.

20. _____ Singapore is his favourite city.

EXERCISE 9.4: CONTINENTS, COUNTRIES, ISLANDS, GROUPS OF ISLANDS

Fill the gap with the or 'no article' (Ø).

1. She really enjoys visiting _____ Asia.

2. My sister is living in _____ Argentina.

3. _____ Corsica is an island in the Mediterranean.

4. _____ New Zealand is really beautiful and green.

5. Would you like to visit _____ Bahamas?

6. Last year we went to _____ Sicily, an Italian island.

7. _____ Canary Islands are popular with tourists.

8. Have you ever been to _____ Azores?

9. _____ Baffin Island is part of Canada.

10. Cairo is the capital of _____ Egypt.

11. I have never been to _____ Africa.

12. Imagine living in _____ Antarctica!

13. _____ Hokkaido is an island in the north of Japan.

14. She travelled all over _____ South America.

15. Do you know where _____ Cook Islands are?

16. Have you ever been to _____ China?

17. How many countries are there in _____ Europe?

18. In _____ Australia there are quite a lot of snakes.

19. _____ Maldives are popular with honeymoon couples.

20. She visited _____ Long Island last summer.

Part 9.3: Places in a city

9.3.1 'No article'

Place	Example	Exceptions
Areas in a city	I've lived in Ø Fulham for five years. They visited a restaurant in Ø Manhattan. She would love a house in Ø Montmartre.	Areas whose name is made up of normal words often need *the*: **the** West End, **the** Lower East Side, **the** Left Bank.
Parks (We often say 'the park' when we're not using its name. See Part 4.1)	Shall we go to Ø Central Park this afternoon? You can see deer in Ø Richmond Park.	

Stations (Note that we say 'the station' when not using its name. See Part 4.4)	I met my friend at Ø Victoria (Station). Our train leaves from Ø Grand Central (Station).	
Airports (We also say 'the airport' when we're not using its name. See Part 4.4).	We flew from Ø Heathrow (Airport). He arrived at Ø Charles de Gaulle (Airport).	
Shops	I love shopping at Ø Harrods. You can buy things very cheaply in Ø Primark.	Shop names that include the word 'shop' often need *the*: **the** Body Shop.
Bridges	Have you been to Ø Tower Bridge? She lives near Ø Hammersmith Bridge. He takes the bus over Ø Putney Bridge every morning.	**The** Forth Road Bridge, **the** Golden Gate Bridge.
Roads, streets, squares	He really hates shopping on Ø Oxford Street. Our school is on Ø Chesilton Road. How do I get to Ø Trafalgar Square?	**The** Strand, **the** King's Road. Roads with numbers in the UK usually have *the*: **the** M1, **the** B32.
Churches and synagogues (See also Part 7.3)	Ø St Paul's Cathedral was designed by Sir Christopher Wren. She got married in Ø All Saints' Church. He attends Ø Bevis Marks Synagogue in London.	Other religious buildings such as mosques and temples often need *the* if the name includes the word 'mosque' or 'temple' but this is not always true and it's best to learn each example individually.

| Schools, colleges (See also Part 7.3) | He works at Ø Birkbeck College.

The children went to Ø Westminster School. | |

9.3.2 *The*

Place	Example	Exceptions
Museums and art galleries	You must go to **the** British Museum. He took his nephew to **the** Science Museum. There is a new exhibition at **the** National Gallery.	Ø Tate Modern.
Hotels	Have you ever had tea at **the** Ritz? I believe he's staying at **the** Dorchester. **The** Savoy is famous for its cocktails.	Hotels with possessive-form names usually have 'no article': Ø Claridge's, Ø Brown's.
Theatres	The play is on at **the** National Theatre. She often goes to **the** Royal Opera House. Have you ever been to **the** Criterion?	Theatres with possessive-form names need 'no article': Ø St. Martin's Theatre.
Pubs (Note that we often say 'the pub' when we're not using its name. See Part 4.2)	We went to **the** Crown and Anchor. They met at **the** King's Head.	Pubs with possessive-form names need 'no article: Ø Molly Mogg's.

9.3.3 Either 'no article' or *the*

	THE	NO ARTICLE
Universities	The University of --- She studied at **the** University of Cambridge.	--- University She studied at Ø Cambridge University.
Cinemas	Cinemas with no place name: We saw the new film at **the** Odeon. He went to **the** IMAX.	Cinemas that include a place name: We saw the new film at Ø Curzon Soho. He went to Ø Cambridge Vue.
Libraries	Libraries which include an adjective: I love working in **the** British Library.	Libraries which include a place name: I borrow a lot of books from Ø Wimbledon Library.
Restaurants and cafés	Restaurant names made up of normal words: I'd love to eat at **the** Fat Duck. Restaurant names that include *the* (these have to be learned individually): We had dinner at **The** Wolseley.	Most other restaurants: Ø Wagamama is my favorite restaurant in London. We had dinner at Ø Pizza Hut. He loves eating in Ø Chipotle. We had coffee in Ø Starbucks.

EXERCISE 9.5

Fill the gap with the or 'no article'(Ø).

1. Have you visited _____ Transport Museum?

2. She stayed in _____ Savoy [hotel] when she was in London.

3. He studied at _____ King's College.

4. I've never been to _____ National Theatre.

5. We ate dinner in _____ Chinatown [area].

6. _____ Westminster Abbey [church] is very beautiful.

7. She works in _____ Victoria and Albert Museum.

8. The play is on at _____ St Martin's Theatre.

9. I live in _____ Chelsea [area].

10. _____ Globe [theatre] is near to the river.

11. Let's meet outside _____ Fulham Library [Fulham is an area in London].

12. We visited _____ University of Oxford.

13. I love having dinner in _____ Claridge's [hotel].

14. _____ Stansted [airport] is quite far from the city.

15. She walked across _____ Wandsworth Bridge.

16. They stopped for a drink at _____ Dog and Fox [pub].

17. She got married in _____ All Saints' Church.

18. _____ National Gallery is enormous.

19. I went to see the new film at _____ Odeon [cinema].

20. Maybe we can stay at _____ Brown's [hotel].

21. He studies at _____ Westminster School.

22. _____ Notting Hill is an expensive part of London.

23. _____ Regent's Park is beautiful in the summer.

24. _____ Criterion [theatre] is in central London.

25. The train leaves from _____ Euston [station].

26. I live near _____ Putney Bridge.

27. _____ Harvey Nichols [shop] has some beautiful things.

28. I go to _____ King's Cross [station] to get the train to Scotland.

29. Let's go to _____ Hyde Park on Sunday.

30. She met me at _____ Gatwick [airport].

Part 9.4: People's names

9.4.1 'No article'

We generally use 'no article' with people's names:

- This is Ø Mr Brown.
- My sister's name is Ø Susan Jenkins.

We also use 'no article' when we address people using common nouns:

- What should I do, Ø Doctor?
- Good morning, Ø children.
- Ø Girls! It's time for dinner!

In the same way, we use 'no article' with familiar names, such as 'Mum', 'Grandpa' and so on:

- Ø Dad's at work just now.
- Ø Granny, can I have a biscuit?
- Ø Aunt Mary and Ø Uncle David have invited us to lunch on Sunday.

9.4.2 *The*

When we are talking about a family, we can use *the + surname + s*:

- **The** Smith**s** are coming to dinner [= Mr and Mrs Smith are coming to dinner].
- We've been invited to go on holiday with **the** Black**s** [= ...with Mr and Mrs Black and their children].

We can also use *the* (we usually stress it if we're speaking) when we want to emphasise that we met the famous person with a certain name:

- I met George Clooney last night. THE George Clooney! [= I met the famous actor, not another person with the same name.]

- She went to school with THE David Beckham!

It's also possible to use *the* when choosing a specific person from a group of people with the same name:

- There are two girls called Lucy in my class. Do you mean **the** tall Lucy with the dark hair or **the** short, blonde Lucy with glasses?

- **The** William that I know would never do such a thing!

We can also do this with cities or countries that don't usually take *the*:

- **The** London of today is so different from **the** London that I lived in when I was growing up.

- My sister's gone on a business trip to Georgia – **the** American Georgia, not **the** Georgia near Russia.

9.4.3 *A/an*

We can use *a/an* before a name to show that we don't know the person or to show that we are a bit uncertain about their identity:

- **A** Mr Thompson called for you.

- There's **a** Jane Green at the door.

We can use *a/an* (often + adjective) before a famous person's name to show that we are saying that someone is a bit like the famous person:

- He's **a** little Einstein (= he's intelligent).
- She's always writing. She's **a** proper Jane Austen.

When we use an artist's name to mean a work of art created by that person, then it behaves like a normal noun:

- She bought **a** Van Gogh [= a painting by Van Gogh]. It cost millions of dollars.

- She has Ø Picassos and Ø Monets in the bank vault [= she has paintings by Picasso and paintings by Monet in the bank vault].

- I love **the** Botticelli that I saw in Florence.

- He practised drawing by copying **the** da Vinci that is in the Louvre in Paris.

In the same way, we can use a writer's name to mean a book by that writer:

- Could you give me **the** Dickens on the table?

EXERCISE 9.6

Choose *the*, *a/an* or 'no article'(Ø).

1. He's so rich that he has _____ Van Gogh in his house.

2. When she was in the US, she met Barack Obama! _____ Barack Obama!

3. _____ Miss Smith called last night [I don't know Miss Smith].

4. Even though it's small, the museum has several Monets and _____ Rembrandt.

5. Could you please pick up _____ Mr Black at the airport? [We know Mr Black].

6. Louise is a bit of _____ Einstein, isn't she? She always gets full marks on the tests.

7. We went on holiday with _____ Bells [Mr and Mrs Bell and their children].

8. My boss's name is _____ John Brown.

9. There's _____ Mr Jones here to see you [I don't know Mr Jones].

10. They had a dinner party and invited _____ Browns [Mr and Mrs Brown].

Section 9 Review Exercises

EXERCISE 9.7

Choose *the*, *a/an* or 'no article'(Ø).

1. I love the fountains in _____ Trafalgar Square.

2. They had a holiday by _____ Lake Geneva.

3. She went hiking in _____ Alps.

4. My son is studying at _____ University of Edinburgh.

5. She hiked near _____ Lake Titicaca.

6. Your son is _____ proper little Picasso! He's very good at drawing.

7. She loved _____ da Vinci that she saw in Paris, so she bought a print of it.

8. A Tale of Two Cities was written by _____ Charles Dickens.

9. We went to _____ Spain last year.

10. _____ St Paul's Cathedral [church] is a very impressive building.

11. She flew over _____ Sahara Desert.

12. Mount Cook is in _____ New Zealand.

13. She spent the winter in _____ Hokkaido, an island in Japan.

14. We can take the train to France from _____ St Pancras [station].

15. I love looking out across _____ Atlantic Ocean.

16. She grew up in _____ Africa.

17. Her plane lands at _____ Heathrow [airport].

18. _____ Thames is the river that runs through London.

19. I really love _____ Richmond Park

20. We didn't stop near _____ Rocky Mountains when we were travelling.

21. _____ Oxford Street gets very busy at the weekends.

22. He saw _____ Michelangelo for the first time when he was in Italy.

23. There's a letter here from _____ Lucy Brown [I don't know Lucy Brown].

24. I've never eaten at _____ Nobu [restaurant].

25. Europeans often go on holiday near _____ Mediterranean.

EXERCISE 9.8

Choose *the*, *a/an* or 'no article'(Ø).

1. She visited _____ Peru last May.

2. _____ Tower Bridge looks amazing at night.

3. Julie would love to travel around _____ California.

4. _____ Canary Islands are part of Spain.

5. _____ National Theatre shows a lot of good plays.

6. They rented a house in _____ Tuscany for the summer.

7. We met her near _____ Prince Charles Cinema

8. I'd love to be able to stay at _____ Ritz [hotel]

9. I often drink coffee in _____ Caffè Nero [café]

10. Have you been to _____ National Portrait Gallery yet ?

11. I saw _____ Mount Fuji from the plane as I was leaving Tokyo.

12. Her cousin went to _____ London University.

13. Could you pass _____ Austen that's on the table, please?

14. He stayed with _____ Fords when he went to New York [Mr and Mrs Ford].

15. She stayed in _____ Taipei for two weeks.

16. We travelled around _____ Asia for our honeymoon.

17. We went shopping in _____ Harrods [shop].

18. The town is close to _____ Great Victoria Desert.

19. _____ Science Museum is great for children.

20. There was an auction of _____ Caravaggio [painting].

21. _____ Helena called earlier. She left you a message [I know Helena].

22. Last night I was sitting next to David Beckham at the cinema. _____ David Beckham!

23. _____ Mississippi flows through New Orleans.

24. Have you ever been to _____ Rio de Janeiro?

25. She lives in _____ Bahamas.

(Remember that you can download all the exercises as printable PDFs at www.perfect-english-grammar.com/a-and-the.html.)

Section 10: Review Exercises

Choose the correct article. Sometimes more than one is possible. If you need help, look at the part of the book listed next to the question in the answer section.

REVIEW EXERCISE 10.1

1. The cold winter has been difficult for _____ elderly.

2. My grandmother goes to _____ church twice a week.

3. John wants _____ new shoes.

4. I went to _____ supermarket that my mother suggested.

5. Give me _____ glass by the chair, please.

6. He spends all his time at _____ gym!

7. My boss and I almost always see eye to _____ eye. It's great to work with someone who has similar ideas.

8. I go to the hairdresser's twice _____ year.

9. We received _____ presents at Christmas.

10. She learned _____ English at school.

11. We often eat lamb on _____ Easter Sunday.

12. Do you call your mother on _____ Mother's Day?

13. Scotland is _____ coldest in January.

14. He studied at _____ University of London.

15. Let's meet on _____ Tuesday afternoon.

16. They always travelled by _____ car during their holiday.

17. The new railway line crosses the country from _____ east to _____ west.

18. Tourists usually visit _____ St Paul's Cathedral in London.

19. She loves seeing films at _____ Prince Charles Cinema.

20. What _____ lovely necklace!

REVIEW EXERCISE 10.2

1. We went to _____ Sicily last year.

2. I saw them walking _____ arm in _____ arm.

3. He won a prize for dancing _____ tango.

4. The government is trying to lower _____ unemployment.

5. Lucy had _____ headache and went to bed early.

6. I've never been to _____ Bali [an island in Indonesia].

7. _____ Nile is the longest river in the world.

8. In New York, many people jog in _____ Central Park.

9. She bought _____ new handbag.

10. I had _____ flu last year and was off work for two weeks.

11. I had _____ piece of cake and _____ cup of coffee.

12. A sloe is a kind of _____ fruit.

13. Do you know much about _____ history of India?

14. He writes about _____ rich and famous for a magazine.

15. She gave me _____ last chocolate.

16. I've read _____ book that our professor lent me.

17. She ate _____ cakes that her brother had made.

18. She has _____ few books – she wishes she could afford more.

19. Could you lend me _____ pen?

20. Leonardo da Vinci died in _____ sixteenth century.

REVIEW EXERCISE 10.3

1. I'd like to go to a restaurant for _____ change. We always eat at home.

2. _____ more you study, _____ better your exam result will be.

3. She likes to stop for a coffee on the way to work in _____ morning.

4. He got _____ hiccups and they lasted all afternoon.

5. I'm interested in _____ history of Africa.

6. Have you flown across _____ Pacific?

7. She loves _____ fourteenth-century art.

8. I love _____ cheese.

9. I've never been to _____ Portugal.

10. I thought she was going to come early but, on _____ contrary, she's already thirty minutes late.

11. After class, Lucy went _____ home and called her boyfriend.

12. _____ Swiss make great chocolate.

13. We saw that film _____ last month.

14. There's _____ fantastic restaurant near her flat.

15. I arrived in Mexico in _____ April.

16. We had sandwiches and Coke for lunch. _____ Coke was warm, though.

17. We met at _____ Victoria Station.

18. I need _____ cup of tea!

19. I'm feeling a bit under _____ weather, so I don't think I'll come to the party tonight.

20. It costs _____ hundred pounds.

REVIEW EXERCISE 10.4

1. Julie is _____ teacher.

2. What will life be like in _____ twenty-second century?

3. Could I use _____ internet at your place?

4. I want to talk to him _____ face to _____ face.

5. My daughter is still at _____ school – she's only fifteen.

6. She hates _____ mushrooms.

7. Lucy bought _____ dress that you recommended.

8. I'll take the exam again _____ next spring.

9. _____ problem is, the weather will be really cold in December.

10. English articles are as easy as _____ pie! I haven't made any mistakes with this exercise.

11. _____ hotter the curry, _____ more Richard eats!

12. Have you ever tried playing _____ rugby?

13. They are _____ Muslims.

14. Do you like _____ French cheese?

15. I travel around London by _____ underground.

16. I went to a party on _____ New Year's Eve.

17. Let's go out tonight – I'd love to see a play at _____ National Theatre.

18. _____ big lorries are very noisy and can damage the roads.

19. I'm going to my yoga class on _____ Thursday morning.

20. I often go to _____ park during the summer.

REVIEW EXERCISE 10.5

1. My mother often goes to _____ Canary Islands on holiday.

2. They are all _____ very good students.

3. _____ Scotch beef is very popular here.

4. I don't know exactly when I'll finish my course – but sometime in _____ next year.

5. Do you speak _____ Spanish?

6. He drank _____ water.

7. She's studying _____ music at college.

8. We wrote an essay about _____ environment.

9. _____ children should go to school.

10. I wrote her address on _____ back of an envelope.

11. Let's go into _____ town this afternoon and go to the cinema.

12. I watched _____ CNN all night.

13. There's _____ wallet on the grass.

14. Who would like to try _____ question 10?

15. Do you do anything special on _____ Christmas Eve?

16. _____ wind howled round the house all night.

17. We have _____ little in the fridge – I think we should go out for dinner.

18. There is a good café near _____ jail.

19. _____ university in Cambridge is very beautiful.

20. We meet for coffee twice _____ week.

REVIEW EXERCISE 10.6

1. My flat is absolutely tiny – there's no room to swing _____ cat.

2. We met in _____ café.

3. She became _____ queen in 1952.

4. What do you think of _____ life abroad?

5. _____ lions are very dangerous.

6. _____ flamingos are pink and white.

7. _____ Mount Fuji is a very beautiful mountain.

8. Richmond Park is _____ biggest park in London.

9. He was elected _____ president last year.

10. He's very keen on _____ baseball.

11. She's interested in _____ music of the 1970s.

12. Her birthday is _____ July 21st.

13. What would you like for _____ lunch?

14. Which is _____ biggest city in the world?

15. John and Lucy finally tied _____ knot last week and they're going on honeymoon to Mexico tomorrow.

16. Amanda's _____ doctor.

17. What are you doing at _____ weekend? Would you like to have lunch?

18. What _____ cold water!

19. My brother was born in _____ 1980s.

20. _____ bigger the cake, _____ better I like it!

REVIEW EXERCISE 10.7

1. I went to the train station early on _____ purpose. I knew it would be very busy.

2. The thief is in _____ court today.

3. I've never been keen on _____ dogs.

4. _____ lions hunt in groups.

5. Sorry, that's _____ wrong answer.

6. She often gives money to _____ homeless.

7. We need to learn about _____ history of China.

8. She's interested in _____ animals.

9. Could you look for _____ large rug at the shops?

10. I loved _____ Barcelona.

11. When I was a child, we always dressed up for _____ Halloween.

12. They climbed part of the way up _____ Everest.

13. At 1 a.m. she finally called it _____ day, and went to bed.

14. She sent the bill by _____ email.

15. On _____ whole, I like travelling, even if occasionally it can get a bit lonely.

16. Please turn to _____ section 7 of your exam paper.

17. I want to buy _____ big house near the river. Do you know of any that are for sale?

18. She has a shower once _____ day.

19. What's the answer to _____ question 5?

20. The North Pole is in _____ Arctic.

REVIEW EXERCISE 10.8

1. I like going to _____ mountains on holiday, but my husband prefers _____ beach.

2. He's reading about _____ NATO.

3. I kept in _____ touch with my classmates for years after we met.

4. Julie and Lucy are _____ very nice girls.

5. We had dinner in a restaurant last night. _____ waitress was very friendly.

6. I went to a hotel on holiday and I really enjoyed swimming in _____ pool.

7. What _____ fantastic party!

8. He sat down on _____ chair and put his feet on _____ stool [there's one chair and one stool near us].

9. What language do _____ Lithuanians speak?

10. They went to _____ Himalayas.

11. What _____ spicy food!

12. I'm so tired, I'd like to go to _____ bed – even though it's only lunchtime!

13. She took _____ plane to Paris.

14. Do you know _____ accountant? I need help with my tax forms!

15. Can you play _____ golf?

16. Did he really use to work for _____ FBI?

17. Is this garden open to _____ public?

18. She's going on _____ world tour. I'm so jealous!

19. _____ station is near the park [the station in our town].

20. Is there _____ French speaker at your work? I need someone to translate this document.

REVIEW EXERCISE 10.9

1. I need _____ new car! My old one is about to fall apart.

2. London is _____ best in the summer.

3. _____ sugar is bad for your health.

4. That's _____ only book I own.

5. _____ Moroccans speak French and Arabic.

6. I'm interested in _____ music of Ireland.

7. The government is trying to improve education for _____ young.

8. What's _____ price of a cup of coffee in Moscow?

9. She went out for dinner with her husband on _____ Valentine's Day.

10. We went to _____ Chelsea [an area of London] and had breakfast in a lovely café.

11. I dropped a cup and a glass. _____ glass smashed.

12. John's _____ vegetarian.

13. There was a sofa in _____ middle of the floor.

14. David's _____ professor.

15. I had _____ cold and couldn't go to work for a week.

16. She loves _____ nature and being outside.

17. I had _____ piano lesson this morning.

18. What do Jewish people do during _____ Passover?

19. They celebrate _____ Chinese New Year.

20. I love looking at _____ moon on a clear night.

REVIEW EXERCISE 10.10

1. She only wears _____ red shoes.

2. I usually take _____ train to Scotland.

3. She bought _____ rice and _____ vegetables.

4. _____ Colombians tend to like socialising.

5. I love reading _____ Spanish poetry.

6. They speak _____ French very well indeed.

7. Could you move your luggage please? It's in _____ way.

8. He's _____ architect.

9. Please close _____ window [there's only one open in the room].

10. _____ poor sometimes don't have good access to education.

11. My plane arrives at _____ Heathrow [airport] about 6 a.m.

12. She's from _____ UK.

13. His birthday is in _____ October.

14. It's lovely to have _____ trees in cities.

15. Do you prefer _____ city or _____ country?

16. He's studying _____ Hindi.

17. He loves _____ music of Africa.

18. I went to Scotland at _____ Christmas.

19. My brother's _____ surgeon.

20. Lucy is _____ cleverest girl I know.

REVIEW EXERCISE 10.11

1. Let's meet in _____ café next to the station.

2. What _____ delicious pasta!

3. She's going to visit Budapest _____ next week.

4. There's _____ nice café in my hometown.

5. I have _____ same dress as you.

6. She goes to _____ cinema every month.

7. We had a cup of coffee in _____ cafeteria at university [there's only one cafeteria there so the listener knows which one I mean].

8. She studied _____ history of Europe.

9. The plane leaves from _____ Gate 25.

10. We went to _____ theatre all the time when we were students.

11. Do you ever go to _____ zoo? I love the penguins!

12. What _____ beautiful garden!

13. Lucy works as _____ hairdresser.

14. _____ college is on King Street.

15. Hand me _____ knives and forks, please [the knives and forks on the table].

16. This new centre is a place where _____ unemployed can come for help and support.

17. She went shopping on _____ Oxford Street, but it was very busy.

18. _____ kittens drink milk.

19. My son David had _____ temperature, so we took him to the doctor.

20. Do you like _____ athletics?

REVIEW EXERCISE 10.12

1. Could you come on _____ 31st of October?

2. Gordon can play _____ piano really well.

3. She went to school on _____ foot.

4. Can anyone play _____ guitar?

5. My parents are _____ accountants.

6. Does she visit her family during _____ Ramadan?

7. Have you read _____ newspaper this morning?

8. Their house is by _____ Indian Ocean.

9. I bought three plants and some pots at the garden centre. I put _____ plants in my garden.

10. Do you drink _____ coffee?

11. I'd like _____ cup of tea.

12. I went to Scotland _____ last Christmas.

13. Do you have _____ internet access at home?

14. There's a test at _____ end of the course.

15. My favourite month is _____ May.

16. She buys her stamps from _____ post office.

17. He got a new laptop and a phone last year. _____ phone has already broken.

18. We ordered lunch in a café. _____ sandwiches were delicious.

19. I bought a new bicycle last week. _____ wheels are red.

20. There's _____ beautiful dress in that shop.

REVIEW EXERCISE 10.13

1. There are at least _____ million people living there.

2. _____ penguins live in cold places.

3. He got married on _____ 5th of April.

4. She's from _____ Bogotá.

5. I'm _____ student.

6. _____ swans have babies called cygnets.

7. The adverts were sent by _____ post.

8. That sounds like _____ tractor!

9. She loves playing _____ tennis.

10. This is _____ coldest winter in a long time.

11. It must have been amazing to be an artist in Italy during _____ Renaissance.

12. Shall we meet on _____ Tuesday?

13. He studies _____ German philosophy.

14. I often fall asleep on _____ bus and miss my stop.

15. I like reading _____ Russian novels.

16. _____ fact is, I don't really like chocolate.

17. Lucy is often on _____ phone.

18. I'm _____ happiest when I'm sitting in the sunshine.

19. He went to _____ hospital to visit his friend.

20. London is _____ exciting city.

REVIEW EXERCISE 10.14

1. _____ British don't seem to mind the weather in the UK.

2. She did her master's degree at _____ Cambridge University.

3. She has _____ few books – they look good on the shelf.

4. I had toast and coffee for _____ breakfast today.

5. The speed limit is 30 miles _____ hour.

6. Lucy was in such _____ hurry she forgot to lock the door.

7. Julie can speak _____ Japanese fluently.

8. Do you know if there's _____ good café near here?

9. She loves having coffee outside in _____ sunshine.

10. I don't like travelling at _____ night.

11. A solicitor is a kind of _____ lawyer.

12. You can open an account at _____ bank.

13. She had _____ cough all winter.

14. Could you write the answer to _____ number 8 on the board please?

15. Shall we have _____ dinner at eight?

16. Is there _____ FAQ on the website?

17. Let's have a cup of coffee in _____ Starbucks.

18. I could see at _____ glance that the flat had been burgled.

19. The train on _____ platform 4 is for London.

20. That film is _____ comedy.

REVIEW EXERCISE 10.15

1. She was an interpreter for _____ UN.

2. She learned to play _____ flute when she was at school.

3. The book will be published in _____ September.

4. Pass me _____ book on the floor.

5. She had _____ measles when she was a child.

6. He played _____ saxophone in a band.

7. She picked up the wrong coat by _____ mistake.

8. His house is near _____ Thames [the river in London].

9. We travelled around _____ South America for six months.

10. We had afternoon tea at _____ Dorchester [a hotel].

11. School children in London often go to _____ British Museum.

12. I listened to the tennis match on _____ radio.

13. She spent two weeks travelling around _____ Tuscany [a region in Italy].

14. She looks like _____ gymnast.

15. We sat by the fire and listened to _____ rain.

16. I'm looking for _____ pair of small, black shoes. I'm going to go shopping tomorrow.

17. There's _____ little milk left – enough for our coffee.

18. She was appointed _____ CEO in March.

19. I usually arrive at _____ work about nine in the morning.

20. _____ cats like chasing _____ mice.

(Remember that you can download all the exercises as printable PDFs at www.perfect-english-grammar.com/a-and-the.html.)

Appendix 1: Pronunciation

When to choose *a* or *an*

We choose either a or an depending on the pronunciation of the next word. We use *a* before consonant sounds, and *an* before vowel sounds. Remember, it's the sound of the word after *a* or *an* which is important, not the spelling, so we say:

- 'a university' /ə juːnɪˈvɜːsɪti/

but (even though it also starts with *U*)

- 'an umbrella' /ən ˌʌmˈbrɛ.lə/

Some more (strange) examples:

- a European country
- a uniform
- an hour
- an honest man

APPENDIX EXERCISE A1.1

Choose *a* or *an*.

1. _____ Easter egg
2. _____ European holiday
3. _____ umbrella
4. _____ yellow dress
5. _____ car
6. _____ beautiful view
7. _____ hour
8. _____ uniform
9. _____ orange
10. _____ interesting day
11. _____ sofa
12. _____ ugly picture
13. _____ expensive suit
14. _____ clever student

15. _____ university library		16. _____ child	
17. _____ good teacher		18. _____ original idea	
19. _____ park		20. _____ useful book	

How to pronounce *the*

The also changes its pronunciation depending on the following word. It's usually pronounced /ðə/ but changes to /ði/ in many accents before a vowel.

Before a consonant sound *the* = /ðə/

- the /ðə/ station

Before a vowel sound *the* = /ði/

- the /ði/ Earth

Names of letters

When we use an article before the names of letters, again we decide if we should use *a* or *an* by the first sound in the name. (Be careful! We don't necessarily use *an* with vowels and *a* with consonants). So with the letter 'M', for example, we use *an*, because the name of the letter M is pronounced /ɛm/. This means that abbreviations such as MP (Member of Parliament) also have *an*: 'I met **an** MP today.'

- Letters which take *an*: A, E, F, H, I, L, M, N, O, R, S, X.
- Letters which take *a*: B, C, D, G, J, K, P, Q, T, U, V, W, Y, Z.

APPENDIX EXERCISE A1.2

Fill the gap with *a* or *an*.

1. The teacher wrote _____ 'A' on the student's work.

2. You can print _____ PDF.

3. She got _____ iPod for her birthday.

4. My brother drives _____ BMW.

5. Her name is Gillian with _____ G.

6. She has _____ IQ of 160.

7. The lecturer gave the student _____ 'F'.

8. I bought _____ CD.

9. He thought he saw _____ UFO.

10. There's _____ ATM round the corner.

(Remember that you can download all the exercises as printable PDFs at www.perfect-english-grammar.com/a-and-the.html.)

Appendix 2: Classification Of Nouns

Common and proper nouns

In most of this book we talk about **common nouns** (these are normal nouns like *rice*, *chair*, *love*, etc.), which follow rules (with some exceptions). **Proper nouns**, which are the names of places and people (these usually have capital letters, like *London*, *John*, *Sydney Opera House*), don't follow so many rules and sometimes the article use just needs to be learned. We talk about proper nouns in Section 9. Usually, the article that we use with proper nouns doesn't change, except in very special circumstances. We (almost) never say 'the London' or 'a London', but always 'London', so once you have learned which article goes with which proper noun then you don't need to think about it again.

APPENDIX EXERCISE A2.1

What kind of nouns are these?

1. Mrs Brown   a: common noun   b: proper noun
2. Library   a: common noun   b: proper noun
3. London   a: common noun   b: proper noun
4. Dog   a: common noun   b: proper noun
5. Chicago   a: common noun   b: proper noun
6. Spain   a: common noun   b: proper noun
7. Houses   a: common noun   b: proper noun
8. Nile   a: common noun   b: proper noun
9. Chair   a: common noun   b: proper noun
10. Money   a: common noun   b: proper noun

Countable and uncountable nouns

There are two types of common noun: **countable** and **uncountable**. It's very important to know the difference!

Countable nouns are often things which can be counted, for example, *book, footballer, bus*. They usually change their form when we make a plural, and can be used with either a singular or a plural verb:

- one book, two book**s**
- one bus, two bus**es**

On the other hand, uncountable nouns are often things which can't easily be counted, like *love, rice* or *happiness*. (But take care! The nouns that are considered countable or uncountable may be different in your language). Uncountable nouns do not change their form, and they are always used with a singular verb. They **usually can't** be used with *a/an*. For example:

- rice [not ~~'one rice, two rices'~~]
- happiness [not ~~'one happiness, two happinesses'~~]
- Rice is delicious [not ~~'rice are delicious'~~].
- Happiness is hard to find [not ~~'happiness are hard to find'~~].

We use *much* and *little* with uncountable nouns, and *many* and *few* with countable nouns. We can use *a lot of / lots of* with both countable and uncountable nouns.

List of common uncountable nouns:

Be careful with these – they might not be uncountable in your language!

air	applause	assistance
baggage	cash	chaos
clothing	concrete	cotton
cutlery	dirt	dust
electricity	equipment	evidence
fabric	fog	fuel

fun	furniture	happiness
harm	health	help
homework	housework	housing
information	knowledge	leisure
lotion	luck	luggage
metal	money	news
oil	paint	pasta
patience	petrol	plastic
progress	publicity	rain
research	rice	rubbish
safety	salt	sand
shopping	smoke	snow
soil	spaghetti	spinach
toothpaste	traffic	transport
travel	truth	violence
weather	wool	work

APPENDIX EXERCISE A2.2

What kind of nouns are these?

1. book   a: singular countable / b: plural countable / c: uncountable

2. countries   a: singular countable / b: plural countable / c: uncountable

3. T-shirts   a: singular countable / b: plural countable / c: uncountable

4. fridge   a: singular countable / b: plural countable / c: uncountable

5. laptops   a: singular countable / b: plural countable / c: uncountable

6. water   a: singular countable / b: plural countable / c: uncountable

7. computers	a: singular countable / b: plural countable / c: uncountable	
8. universes	a: singular countable / b: plural countable / c: uncountable	
9. plates	a: singular countable / b: plural countable / c: uncountable	
10. love	a: singular countable / b: plural countable / c: uncountable	
11. rice	a: singular countable / b: plural countable / c: uncountable	
12. cup	a: singular countable / b: plural countable / c: uncountable	
13. apple	a: singular countable / b: plural countable / c: uncountable	
14. toothbrushes	a: singular countable / b: plural countable / c: uncountable	
15. shoe	a: singular countable / b: plural countable / c: uncountable	
16. tea	a: singular countable / b: plural countable / c: uncountable	
17. train	a: singular countable / b: plural countable / c: uncountable	
18. phones	a: singular countable / b: plural countable / c: uncountable	
19. paint	a: singular countable / b: plural countable / c: uncountable	
20. spaghetti	a: singular countable / b: plural countable / c: uncountable	
21. handbag	a: singular countable / b: plural countable / c: uncountable	
22. steaks	a: singular countable / b: plural countable / c: uncountable	
23. toothpaste	a: singular countable / b: plural countable / c: uncountable	
24. ring	a: singular countable / b: plural countable / c: uncountable	
25. research	a: singular countable / b: plural countable / c: uncountable	
26. weather	a: singular countable / b: plural countable / c: uncountable	
27. watch	a: singular countable / b: plural countable / c: uncountable	
28. chairs	a: singular countable / b: plural countable / c: uncountable	
29. furniture	a: singular countable / b: plural countable / c: uncountable	
30. dust	a: singular countable / b: plural countable / c: uncountable	

APPENDIX EXERCISE A2.3

Are these sentences correct? Change them if they're wrong.

1. We have a lot of homeworks.

2. She does researches at the university.

3. I need a knowledge about history.

4. He had a lot of fun at the party.

5. We need some new furnitures.

6. How many baggages do you have?

7. I need more informations.

8. I hope we have a good weather on holiday.

9. We made a progress with the work.

10. Do you have any cash?

11. The news are good.

12. I need an accommodation for tonight.

13. Can we have spaghettis for dinner?

14. There was a snow last night.

15. Hope you have a good luck!

Special cases

Occasionally, uncountable nouns can be used like countable nouns. This is especially true when we mean 'a portion of'. For example:

- two waters [= 'two glasses of water']
- a coffee [= 'a cup of coffee']

Other normally uncountable nouns used in this way include:

- juice
- tea
- sugar
- curry
- salad

We can also sometimes use uncountable nouns as countable when they mean 'a kind of'. For example:

- a jam [= a kind of jam]

- some jams [= different kinds of jam (raspberry, strawberry etc.)]

Other nouns used in this way include:

- medicine
- bread
- cereal
- fruit
- cheese
- soap

See also Part 7.2 about using 'a/an' with uncountable nouns.

Nouns that can be either countable or uncountable

Some nouns can be either countable or uncountable, depending on the situation. Often they change their meaning completely:

	Countable	*Uncountable*
Hair	One hair: 'There's a hair in my soup!'	All the hair on a person's head: 'You have lovely hair.'
Paper	Newspaper: 'I read two (news)papers every morning.'	Paper for writing on: 'Could you give me some paper, please?'
Chicken	Chicken the animal: 'She keeps chickens in her garden.'	Chicken the food: 'I eat chicken very often.'
Noise	One single instance of noise: 'I heard a noise.'	Noise in general: 'The workmen made a lot of noise.'
Business	One single company: 'She started a business.'	Business in general: 'Business is important for the economy.'

Beauty	A beautiful person: 'She's such a beauty.'	Beauty in general: 'He loves the beauty of the natural world.'
Experience	One event: 'I had a great experience when I was travelling.'	Having done something for a long time: 'She has a lot of experience – she'd be great for this job.'
Light	A lamp: 'I bought a new light for the living room.'	Light in general: 'Light travels very quickly.'
Talk	A lecture: 'We listened to a talk about Plato.'	Discussion in general: 'There was a lot of talk about the new building.'
Lamb	Lamb the animal: 'There are three lambs in the field.'	Lamb the food: 'We had lamb for lunch.'
Sound	A single instance of sound: 'There was a sound in the night.'	Sound in general: 'The speed of sound is less than the speed of light.'
Cloth	A piece of cloth (usually for cleaning): 'Pass me a cloth! I've spilled water everywhere!'	Cloth as a material: 'I bought cloth to make new curtains.'
Cake	A whole cake: 'My mother baked two cakes last night.'	Cake as a mass: 'I've eaten so much cake!'
Yogurt	A pot of yogurt: 'Could you get three yogurts from the fridge?'	Yogurt as a liquid: 'I've spilled yogurt on the carpet!'

APPENDIX EXERCISE A2.4

Are these sentences correct?

1. That actress has lovely hairs.

2. The government is trying to encourage business by reducing taxes.

3. She bought four cheeses.

4. I eat chickens and chips very often.

5. The news is very bad, I'm afraid.

6. The planes make a lot of noises.

7. The lecturer gave talk about art history.

8. She ordered two mineral waters.

9. There were lambs playing in the field.

10. My garden gets a lot of lights.

Appendix 2 Review Exercises

APPENDIX EXERCISE A2.5

Are these sentences correct?

1. She bought me a tea and a slice of cake.

2. You can leave your luggages here.

3. We don't eat many rice at home.

4. I'm looking for an information about hotels.

5. She had a huge selection of different teas.

6. Could I have a coffee?

7. Could you give me an advice?

8. I need an assistance with this.

9. She appreciates beauty.

10. Have you done your homeworks?

11. The traffic were terrible this morning.

12. We haven't made much progress, I'm afraid.

13. She ate yogurt with blueberries.

14. She bought carrots and spinaches.

15. There is a lot of researches into this problem.

16. The money are on the table.

17. There isn't much evidence against the person accused of the crime.

18. Do you have a work?

19. A fun is important, but don't forget to study too.

20. Experience is often more important than qualifications.

(Remember that you can download all the exercises as printable PDFs at www.perfect-english-grammar.com/a-and-the.html.)

Appendix 3: *Some / Any / 'No Article'*

We can use *some*, *any* or 'no article' before plural or uncountable nouns. They all mean something similar to *a/an* before a singular noun. For example:

- Can I have **a** banana? [One banana, but any one is okay.]

- Can I have **some** bananas? [More than one banana, but any small group is okay.]

The difference between *some* and 'no article':

Often, there isn't a big difference in meaning between 'no article' and *some*. However, we use *some* when we are talking about a limited number or amount (but we don't know or we don't want to say the exact quantity).

Some means 'a certain number of' or 'a certain amount of'. We don't use *some* if we are talking about something in general or thinking about it as a category. When we use *some*, we don't say the exact quantity, but we could probably find it out if we needed to. For example:

- Can you buy **some** milk? [We don't know exactly how much, but I'm talking about a certain amount of milk – I don't want all the milk in the world.]

On the other hand, we use 'no article' when we aren't thinking about the quantity. It's used to talk about the noun as a category, rather than a certain amount of it:

- We need Ø milk to make pancakes. [I'm thinking about milk as a category. I'm not thinking about a certain amount of milk.]

More examples:

- We need to buy Ø coffee [I'm talking about coffee as a category, not thinking about the amount].

- Would you like **some** coffee? [I mean a certain amount of coffee, probably a cup.]

- I ate **some** bread [I mean a certain amount of bread].

- I ate Ø bread [not pasta or rice].

Remember that often it doesn't make a big difference:

- Do you want Ø tea? [I'm not thinking about the amount.]

- Do you want **some** tea? [I'm thinking about the amount, but the meaning is really the same as the first sentence.]

APPENDIX EXERCISE A3.1

Fill the gap with *some* or 'no article' (Ø).

1. Can you buy _____ pasta? [I'm thinking of the amount we need for tonight.]

2. We need _____ mushrooms [I'm not thinking about the amount].

3. John drinks _____ coffee every morning [coffee, not tea].

4. Add _____ water to the soup if it's too thick [a certain amount of water].

5. I really want _____ tea – could you get me a cup?

6. We could have _____ rice for dinner [rice, not pasta].

7. I ate _____ bread and two eggs for lunch [I'm thinking about the amount].

8. She bought _____ new furniture [a certain amount of furniture].

9. Did you get _____ carrots? [I'm not thinking about the amount.]

10. I'd like _____ tea, please! [Tea, not juice or coffee.]

The difference between *some* and *any*:

Generally, we use *any* in the same way as *some*: when we are thinking about a certain amount or number of something. Remember, usually both *some* and *any* can only be used with plural countable nouns or uncountable nouns, but **not usually** with singular countable nouns.

We usually use *some* with affirmative (positive) sentences and *any* with negatives and questions:

- She bought **some** tomatoes [positive sentence].

- She didn't buy **any** tomatoes [negative sentence].
- Did she buy **any** tomatoes [question]?

However, there are some exceptions to this.

1. *Any* can be used in a positive sentence to mean 'it's not important which one'. When we use *any* in this way, it's most often used with singular countable nouns:

- You can take **any** bus.
- Pass me **any** glass.
- Come over **any** Sunday.

2. *Any* can also be used in positive sentences that have a negative feeling, for example if they include *never, hardly, without*:

- She never eats **any** fruit.
- We hardly watch **any** television.
- Julia left the house without **any** money.

3. *Some* can be used in questions when we expect that the answer will be 'yes'. This is very common in offers and requests:

- Would you like **some** coffee?
- Do you want **some** sandwiches?
- Could you give me **some** help?
- Could you pass me **some** sugar?

Compare the following two sentences:

- Do you have **any** letters for me? [This is a real question. I don't know if you have any letters or not.]
- Do you have **some** letters for me? [I think you do, so I'm expecting that you will say 'yes'.]

APPENDIX EXERCISE A3.2

Fill the gap with *some* or *any*.

1. Have we got _____ bread? [A real question, I have no idea.]

2. _____ student will tell you that they don't have enough money [it doesn't matter which student].

3. We've got _____ furniture, but we still need a table.

4. She bought _____ new clothes.

5. You can buy beer in _____ pub [it doesn't matter which pub].

6. Can I have _____ more juice? [I expect you will say 'yes'.]

7. Did you buy _____ juice? [I have no idea, this is a real question.]

8. I can speak _____ French.

9. Would you like _____ tea? [An offer – I think you will say 'yes'.]

10. In London in the winter there's hardly _____ sunlight.

11. Go into _____ shop on the high street and ask [it doesn't matter which shop].

12. Would you like _____ more meat? [An offer – I think you will say 'yes'.]

13. There's _____ money in my handbag.

14. Did you buy _____ chicken? [I expect you will say 'yes', because we talked about it before.]

15. I don't have _____ sunblock with me.

16. She never drinks _____ water.

17. Do you have _____ sugar? [I expect you will say 'yes', because usually you have sugar.]

18. It's hard in a new city without _____ friends.

19. I didn't find _____ problems.

20. Could you give me _____ paper? [A request – I expect you will say 'yes'.]

(Remember that you can download all the exercises as printable PDFs at www.perfect-english-grammar.com/a-and-the.html.)

Answers To Exercises

Answers to Section 2

EXERCISE 2.1

1. Sorry, I've spilled water on **the** book [there's only one book on the table so the listener knows which book].

2. Sorry, I've spilled water on **a** book [there are lots of books on the table, and it's not clear to the listener which book].

3. She needs **a** chair from the dining room [the listener can see that there are several chairs in the dining room].

4. She needs **the** chair from the dining room [the listener can see that there's only one chair in the dining room].

5. Would you mind opening **the** door? [I mean the door of the room we are in.]

6. He walked into **a** door and hit his head [the listener doesn't know which door].

7. She fell into **the** river [there's one river in our town].

8. She fell into **a** river [the listener doesn't know which river – it could be any river in the country].

9. I had dinner in **the** Chinese restaurant [I mean the one near our house].

10. I had dinner in **a** Chinese restaurant [there are hundreds in London and the listener doesn't know which one].

EXERCISE 2.2

1. I drank **the** cup of coffee that I'd just bought.

2. I drank **a** cup of coffee.

3. John's going out with **the** French girl who we met last week.

4. John's going out with **a** French girl.

5. I bought **a** new laptop.

6. I bought **the** laptop that I told you about.

7. David had dinner in **a** restaurant.

8. David had dinner in **the** restaurant that he usually goes to.

9. He played **a** piece of music.

10. He played **the** piece of music that we were discussing yesterday.

EXERCISE 2.3

1. Let's meet in **a** café.

2. Let's meet in **the** café next to my flat.

3. I picked up **the** piece of paper on the floor.

4. I picked up **a** piece of paper.

5. Could you put these flowers on **a** table?

6. Could you put these flowers on **the** table next to the door?

7. I put my new cushion on **a** chair.

8. I put my new cushion on **the** chair next to the fireplace.

9. She bought a new dress in **a** shop.

10. She bought a new dress in **the** shop next to the supermarket.

EXERCISE 2.4

1. Julie crashed her bike into **a** tree.

2. Julie crashed her bike into **the** only tree in her garden.

3. We went to **a** restaurant.

4. We went to **the** usual restaurant.

5. John has **a** yellow car.

6. John has **the** same yellow car as Mike.

7. Let's get **a** taxi.

8. Let's get **the** next taxi.

9. He brought **a** cake.

10. He brought **the** wrong cake.

11. She put down **a** card and won the game.

12. She put down **the** right card and won the game.

EXERCISE 2.5

1. Everest is **the** highest mountain in the world.

2. Who is **the** oldest person in your family?

3. This dress was **Ø** cheapest.

4. Which language do you think is **Ø** easiest to learn?

5. This book is **the** most serious one on the topic.

6. I think that one over there is **the** strongest horse.

7. This film is **Ø** shortest.

8. She's **the** fastest runner in her school.

9. That suitcase is **Ø** lightest.

10. Out of all the cities in Europe, London is **Ø** biggest.

EXERCISE 2.6

1. I read a lot of books on the subject and this one is **the** best.

2. I wake up **Ø** earliest on Mondays, as I go to a yoga class. On other days I sleep later.

3. Amanda's Ø happiest when she's on holiday.

4. Which student in the class is **the** happiest?

5. This juice is Ø most delicious if you chill it for a long time first.

6. The British Library is Ø best in the mornings. It's too crowded in the afternoons.

7. John is Ø calmest when he's working.

8. Of all the people in our office, Adrian is **the** calmest.

9. Lucy wakes up **the** earliest in her family.

10. Which juice is **the** most delicious? Apple juice, orange juice or raspberry juice?

EXERCISE 2.7

1. He gave me **a** clock and **a** picture as a wedding present. **The** clock belonged to his grandmother.

2. I took **a** suitcase and **a** backpack on holiday. **The** suitcase was much more useful.

3. John broke **a** vase when he was in Marie's house. **The** vase was over 100 years old.

4. Julie read **a** book and **a** magazine. She said **the** book was quite boring, though.

5. I washed **a** white shirt and **a** red top together. Now **the** shirt is pink.

EXERCISE 2.8

1. She gave us Ø bread and Ø orange juice. The orange juice was delicious.

2. I got **a** book and **a** magazine from the library.

3. We watched Ø films and Ø TV programmes all night. The films were better.

4. She offered us **a** piece of cake or Ø biscuits.

5. We had Ø broccoli and Ø cheese for dinner.

6. I dropped **a** glass and two bowls. They all broke.

7. We cooked Ø spaghetti and Ø bacon. John had bought the spaghetti in Rome.

8. She has **a** black umbrella and I have **a** blue one. The blue one is much bigger.

9. We had **a** piece of pie and **Ø** potatoes for lunch. The pie was very good indeed.

10. I took **a** bottle of wine and **a** box of chocolates to the party.

11. I drank **a** cup of coffee and ate **Ø** biscuits. The biscuits had been made by my mother.

12. She bought **Ø** shoes and **a** dress to wear to her sister's wedding.

13. Ruth has **a** son and **Ø** two daughters. One of the daughters is in my class.

14. They drank **Ø** water and **Ø** tea.

15. At the weekend, I crashed my bike into **a** car.

16. I moved into **a** new flat last month. It's really lovely.

17. Could you get **Ø** milk and **a** bar of chocolate when you are at the shop?

18. I had **Ø** pasta and **a** glass of wine last night. The pasta was really good.

19. I spilled **Ø** coffee on the sofa and I dropped **a** jug of milk on the floor.

20. John has **Ø** orange chairs and **Ø** green carpets!

EXERCISE 2.9

1. I bought **a** new dress, but I was annoyed to find that **the** zip was broken.

2. They stopped for **a** picnic. However, **the** lemonade was warm.

3. Amelia went to **a** restaurant. She saw **a** famous actress there.

4. She sat down on **a** chair, and started reading **a** book.

5. They hired **a** car on holiday, but when they opened **the** boot, **a** cat was hiding inside!

EXERCISE 2.10

1. William is **the** cutest baby in London.

2. Let's start again from **the** beginning of the song.

3. I bought **a** new dress.

4. Which is your favourite city in **the** world?

5. He was wearing **the** same T-shirt as his brother.

6. I'll meet you in **the** usual place.

7. This is **the** only dress I could find.

8. Today is **the** coldest day of the year.

9. I bought **the** wrong book.

10. He bought a pen and some paper in the shop. **The** pen was red.

11. She crashed her bicycle into a car, and broke **the** windscreen.

12. She lay on her back on the grass and looked at **the** sky.

13. Everest is **the** highest mountain in the world.

14. I had **a** cup of tea and **a** biscuit. They were both delicious.

15. Please pass **the** water jug [there is one water jug on our table].

16. Have you read **the** book that I lent you?

17. I love looking at **the** planets on a clear night.

18. There's **Ø** dirt all over his jeans.

19. What's **the** title of the film that you saw last night?

20. There's **a** post office near the bank.

EXERCISE 2.11

1. The page number is at **the** bottom of each page.

2. How many planets are in **the** solar system?

3. We ate **Ø** sandwiches and drank **Ø** water.

4. I bought a new dress. It has a pattern on **the** sleeves.

5. I had **a** cup of coffee for breakfast.

6. I met a man and a woman last night. **The** woman was from Mexico.

7. She bought **a** new laptop.

8. There are **Ø** people outside.

9. She wants to sit in **the** armchair [there is only one armchair in this room].

10. In the countryside, you can see **the** stars much more clearly than in the city.

11. There's **a** good hairdresser on that road.

12. I had **Ø** bread and cheese for lunch.

13. It's not good for your eyes to look directly at **the** sun.

14. Where's **the** shop that John works in?

15. I've got **a** tent, but it's very old. You can borrow it if you want.

16. They went for a walk and looked at **the** moon.

17. It's on **the** back of the page.

18. She gave me **the** last chocolate.

19. She put **a** book in her bag [you don't know which book].

20. She bought **the** laptop that her brother recommended.

EXERCISE 2.12

1. I had lunch in a lovely restaurant. **The** main course was excellent.

2. Julie has **a** sister and two brothers.

3. Please pass me **the** coffee on the table [there is one cup of coffee and one table near us].

4. Sorry, that's **the** wrong book. I need the one by David Jones.

5. It's amazing to think about how big **the** universe is.

6. John is **the** tallest in his family.

7. There are **Ø** spiders in the bath.

8. We rented **a** car on holiday.

9. She walked into a beautiful house. **The** kitchen was near **the** front door.

10. There's **a** Japanese restaurant near my house.

11. The artist's name is on **the** back of the painting.

12. I bought **a** new computer.

13. My brother is in **the** middle of the photo.

14. She got **Ø** new shoes last weekend.

15. Which is **the** right answer?

16. There's **Ø** luggage in the hall.

17. This is **the** most beautiful painting that I've ever seen.

18. I visited **an** old castle yesterday.

19. I bought a new bicycle, but **the** seat is really uncomfortable.

20. At **the** end of the book, they fell in love.

Answers to Section 3

EXERCISE 3.1

1. He hates **Ø** cats.

2. I like **the** cats that you have.

3. I gave her back **the** books that she'd lent me.

4. **Ø** Books are expensive.

5. **Ø** Rice is very popular in Asia.

6. Pass **the** rice please [it's on our table].

7. It's impressive how clever **Ø** dogs are.

8. **The** dogs that my friend has are really stupid.

9. Many people say that **the** love that you feel for your baby is exceptionally strong.

10. **Ø** Love is more important than money.

11. She loves **Ø** flowers – you could buy her some for her birthday.

12. I put **the** flowers that I received for my birthday in a vase.

13. Ø Chocolate is made from cocoa.

14. She put **the** chocolate that she bought in the fridge.

15. I dropped **the** cakes that you made on the way to the party.

16. She likes making Ø cakes.

17. **The** lions in London Zoo are quite friendly.

18. Ø Lions are very scary animals.

19. Do you think Ø money is important for a happy life?

20. I need **the** money that I left on the table.

EXERCISE 3.2

1. We studied Ø German philosophy.

2. We read about **the** poetry of Scotland.

3. He's interested in Ø human happiness.

4. I took a class on Ø French literature.

5. The book's about **the** music of Ireland.

6. I've never studied **the** art of the Far East.

7. I watched a programme on TV about Ø twentieth-century ideas.

8. She writes about Ø modern art.

9. She's writing her thesis on **the** philosophy of Hegel.

10. I read an article about **the** history of South America.

11. She read a book about **the** philosophy of Kant.

12. He likes Ø eighteenth-century poetry.

13. There was a documentary about **the** literature of the United States.

14. Could you tell me more about Ø Indian music?

15. There was an article in the paper about **Ø** Italian art.

16. He likes discussing **the** ideas of the Greek philosophers.

17. They studied **the** science of the natural world.

18. We listened to a lecture on **the** work of Leonardo da Vinci.

19. They are very interested in **Ø** Chinese calligraphy.

20. We read about **Ø** British history.

EXERCISE 3.3

1. It's important for **a nurse** to be kind and friendly.

2. **Ø Nurses** from all the hospitals in the country went on strike last week.

3. **A car needs** to be cleaned from time to time.

4. **Ø Cars cause** huge environmental problems.

5. **A plant has** roots, stems and leaves.

6. Without **Ø plants**, humans couldn't live.

7. **A tiger eats** meat.

8. **Ø Tigers kill** a few people a year, but most tigers don't attack people.

EXERCISE 3.4

1. **Ø** Young people spend too much time on the internet.

2. **The** young spend too much time on the internet.

3. The government has a duty to protect **the** poor.

4. The government has a duty to protect **Ø** poor people.

5. How can we find work for all **the** unemployed?

6. How can we find work for all **Ø** unemployed people?

7. She works with Ø deaf people.

8. She works with **the** deaf.

9. Is it a good idea to raise taxes for **the** rich?

10. Is it a good idea to raise taxes for Ø rich people?

11. I try to help **the** homeless if I can.

12. I try to help Ø homeless people if I can.

13. It's wrong to exploit **the** weak.

14. It's wrong to exploit Ø weak people.

15. **The** elderly are often lonely.

16. Ø Elderly people are often lonely.

17. This charity helps **the** hungry all over the world.

18. This charity helps Ø hungry people all over the world.

19. This exclusive restaurant is popular with Ø wealthy people.

20. This exclusive restaurant is popular with **the** wealthy.

EXERCISE 3.5

1. **The Scottish** like chocolate.

2. **Kenyans** like chocolate.

3. **Brazilians** like chocolate.

4. **The Chinese** like chocolate.

5. **The Swedish** like chocolate.

6. **Italians** like chocolate.

7. **The Turkish** like chocolate.

8. **The Polish** like chocolate.

9. **Indians** like chocolate.

10. **Australians** like chocolate.

EXERCISE 3.6

1. I love Ø ice cream.

2. We were reading about **the** philosophy of the Middle Ages.

3. I really hate **the** cats on this street.

4. Look at **the** dust on this table!

5. She studied Ø fifteenth-century art.

6. The lecture was about Ø French literature.

7. She loves **the** ice cream that her mother makes.

8. David is allergic to Ø dust.

9. The children are keen on Ø animals.

10. We spent the afternoon learning about **the** novels of the twentieth century.

11. Ø Cigarettes aren't allowed in here.

12. Could you please pass me **the** salt on the table?

13. She loves reading about Ø Chinese philosophy.

14. I don't like **the** animals that my brother has.

15. My mother really hates Ø cats.

16. He talks a lot about **the** art of the fourteenth century.

17. I'm not keen on Ø cheese.

18. Julie loves working with Ø children.

19. Where are **the** keys that I left in the hall?

20. We studied Ø African music.

EXERCISE 3.7

1. Can you teach me about **Ø** Italian food?

2. **The** flowers in that garden are very beautiful.

3. They learned about **Ø** twentieth-century theatre.

4. I really love **Ø** coffee.

5. **The** cakes that my flatmate makes are delicious.

6. **Ø** Young people often have trouble finding jobs these days.

7. **Ø** Money doesn't always lead to **Ø** happiness.

8. She wrote a book about **the** philosophy of the Middle Ages.

9. **Ø** Peace is better than **Ø** war.

10. My brother likes **Ø** chocolate very much.

11. She wrote her thesis about **the** art of the nineteenth century.

12. Many people say that **Ø** teenagers are lazy, but I don't think that's true.

13. Please pass me **the** money on the table.

14. Julie likes **the** coffee that they serve in the café next to her house.

15. I like **the** children who live next door to my house – they are adorable.

16. He really hates **Ø** mushrooms.

17. **The** teenagers that I know all study hard.

18. We shouldn't take **Ø** good health for granted.

19. Could you give John **the** books that I left at your flat?

20. **The** Spanish usually go to bed later than **the** British.

EXERCISE 3.8

1. Julian says that politicians are too hard on **the** poor.

2. **The** Japanese often eat a very healthy diet.

3. She loves Ø Asian food.

4. This charity tries to help **the** hungry in poor countries.

5. How can we provide opportunities for **the** uneducated?

6. **The** Chinese often like green tea.

7. Many processed foods contain Ø palm oil.

8. Are Ø cars a problem?

9. He thinks **the** rich should pay more tax.

10. The Prime Minister is trying to help **the** unemployed.

11. **The** elderly are very powerful politically.

12. She doesn't drink Ø white wine.

13. Ø Black clothes are popular in northern Europe.

14. She thought **the** people of Cambridge were extremely friendly.

15. I really like eating Ø spicy food.

16. This new hotel will be very popular with **the** tourist.

17. Ø Rats can carry disease.

18. In the twenty-first century, Ø employees often work at home.

19. How will this new law affect **the** shopkeeper?

20. Ø Young children need a lot of sleep.

Answers to Section 4

EXERCISE 4.1

1. We travelled by Ø boat when we went on holiday.

2. Laura is on **the** train.

3. How do you get to work? On Ø foot?

4. Can I take **the** train to San Francisco?

5. Get off **the** subway at Central Park North.

6. She went to Paris by **Ø** train.

7. He loves travelling by **Ø** bike.

8. You shouldn't talk loudly while you're on **the** bus.

9. She could take **the** plane to Glasgow.

10. I travel around London by **Ø** bus.

EXERCISE 4.2

1. She sent the information by **Ø** email.

2. Did you hear the news on **the** radio?

3. Could you find out the time of the train by **Ø** phone?

4. The book arrived by **Ø** post.

5. Has **the** mail already arrived?

6. How much time do you spend on **the** phone?

7. The scandal was all over **the** newspapers.

8. Could we advertise by **Ø** mail?

9. These days news is often communicated on the internet and the TV as well as by **Ø** radio.

10. Your document's in **the** post.

EXERCISE 4.3

1. Julie kissed **his** cheek.

2. Julie kissed him on **the** cheek.

3. Julie held **his** arm.

4. Julie held him by **the** arm.

5. Julie patted him on **the** back.

6. Julie patted **his** back.

EXERCISE 4.4

1. What time do you get up in **the** morning?

2. By **Ø** day he's an accountant, but after work he's the drummer in a rock group.

3. We usually study in **the** afternoon.

4. They often go to the pub at **Ø** night.

5. I'm sorry, I can't meet during **the** week. I'm very busy at work at the moment.

6. By **Ø** night, London looks totally different.

7. He works during **the** day.

8. What are you doing at **the** weekend?

9. She met her friends in **the** evening.

10. It's so cold here! Even in **the** daytime, it's below freezing.

EXERCISE 4.5

1. She works for **the** fire brigade.

2. We travelled by **Ø** plane.

3. I really need a holiday at **the** beach!

4. **Ø** Pollution is a major problem in our cities.

5. Shall we go to **the** cinema tonight?

6. I'd love to go to **the** opera.

7. Young people don't know enough about **Ø** literature.

8. He's worried about **Ø** crime.

9. She caught **the** train at King's Cross station.

10. The boss said he would contact Julie by **Ø** phone.

11. We met at **the** pub.

12. Lucy can play **the** violin beautifully.

13. I took **the** bus to the concert.

14. I need to take my son to **the** doctor's today, so I can't come to lunch.

15. I went to the party by **Ø** car.

16. My grandmother refuses to put her money in **the** bank.

17. I'll send you the bill by **Ø** email.

18. I love listening to my husband play **the** cello.

19. I can't meet you in **the** week, as I always work late.

20. She went from Warsaw to London by **Ø** bus.

EXERCISE 4.6

1. I really love listening to **Ø** music.

2. She studies **Ø** philosophy at university.

3. John has played **the** piano since he was a child.

4. She went to **the** ballet on her birthday.

5. Do you like **the** city?

6. He hates swimming in **the** sea, and prefers a swimming pool.

7. Are you interested in **Ø** art?

8. **Ø** Poverty is the biggest problem we need to solve.

9. I bought some bread at **the** baker's.

10. My cousin is sometimes on **the** radio talking about the economy.

11. I took lessons to learn how to play **the** clarinet.

12. To succeed as a writer you need **Ø** luck and good timing.

13. It's easy to get around Paris by **Ø** metro.

14. The parcel will come by **Ø** post.

15. They often visit **the** theatre.

16. You can take **the** underground to the restaurant.

17. I spent two hours on **the** phone last night.

18. There was a programme about **Ø** climate change on TV last night.

19. Listen to **the** wind!

20. She loves **Ø** nature and often goes for long walks in the country.

EXERCISE 4.7

1. She sent the invitation in **the** post.

2. Lucy went for a swim, and then to **the** hairdresser's.

3. We might take **the** boat to France.

4. I'm not rich enough to always travel by **Ø** taxi!

5. Responsibility is important for **Ø** society.

6. If you have toothache, you should go to **the** dentist's.

7. You can exchange money at **the** post office

8. We often go to **the** seaside in summer.

9. My mother lives in **the** countryside.

10. It's important to keep up with **Ø** technology.

11. I love going to university by **Ø** bike.

12. The satellite is in **Ø** space.

13. He travelled around the USA by **Ø** motorbike.

14. I went skiing in **the** mountains.

15. We usually drink tea at around four o'clock in **the** afternoon.

16. Ø Life can be difficult when you don't have much money.

17. London looks much better in **the** sunshine.

18. She travelled around Japan by Ø train.

19. Ø Unemployment has risen recently.

20. We learned about Ø global warming at school.

EXERCISE 4.8

1. She hates **the** city and much prefers to live in a village.

2. How does the government's attitude affect Ø society?

3. She can't come for coffee because she has to go to **the** doctor's.

4. I'd love to live by **the** sea.

5. He explored Argentina by Ø motorbike.

6. Do you spend a lot of time on **the** phone?

7. It's important to be happy in **the** present.

8. My mother thinks I should put all my money in my savings account at **the** bank.

9. In Cambridge, everyone gets around by Ø bike.

10. He listens to **the** radio every night.

11. He's interested in Ø nature and the environment.

12. I really hate going to **the** dentist's.

13. Would you like to travel into Ø space?

14. Shall we go to **the** pub later?

15. He plays **the** piano very well.

16. They travelled from England to Spain by Ø boat.

17. Do you go to work on Ø foot?

18. We went hiking in **the** mountains on holiday.

19. How often do you go to **the** hairdresser's?

20. I need to buy some stamps at **the** post office.

EXERCISE 4.9

1. We travelled around Tokyo by **Ø** underground.

2. Do you often work in **the** evening?

3. She often gets up for a glass of water during **the** night.

4. John needs a new tie because he's going to **the** opera.

5. He goes to work by **Ø** car.

6. The children love **the** seaside.

7. I'd love to visit Brazil in **the** future.

8. We went for a walk and enjoyed **the** sunshine.

9. She lay in bed and listened to **the** wind outside.

10. **Ø** Unemployment is a big problem at the moment.

11. She travelled around California by **Ø** bus.

12. His grandfather thinks that **Ø** climate change is a myth.

13. What shall we do tomorrow? How about going to **the** zoo?

14. The children learn a lot about **Ø** global warming.

15. He likes getting up early and walking to **the** baker's to buy fresh bread.

16. I often go to Scotland by **Ø** plane, although occasionally I drive.

17. She loves playing **the** violin.

18. Many companies are trying to reduce **Ø** pollution.

19. Can your brother play **the** guitar?

20. How can we tackle **Ø** poverty?

EXERCISE 4.10

1. The bill will come in **the** post.

2. Did you take **the** bus home yesterday?

3. You need **Ø** luck and skill to win.

4. How often do you go to **the** cinema?

5. He usually takes **the** plane when he goes to Paris.

6. How can we use **Ø** technology to improve everybody's life?

7. A friend of mine took **the** train all the way across Russia.

8. The valley looks beautiful in **the** rain.

9. She loves going to **the** theatre.

10. I try not to sleep in **the** daytime.

11. She spends a lot of time listening to **Ø** music.

12. We often go to **the** ballet.

13. Last week, we went to a lecture about **Ø** history.

14. That's **Ø** life!

15. She loves **the** beach and takes a holiday by the Mediterranean at least twice a year.

16. We studied **the** present perfect tense in my English class today.

17. She sent the money by **Ø** post.

18. His brother plays **the** piano beautifully.

19. She really knows how to dance **the** tango.

20. How will **the** public react to this new law?

EXERCISE 4.11

1. We did **the** foxtrot all night.

2. Did you come by **Ø** taxi?

3. He usually goes to work by **Ø** underground.

4. I like to get up early in **the** morning.

5. The Prime Minister promised to reduce **Ø** crime.

6. What do you like to do at **the** weekend?

7. Can you imagine what it was like to live in **the** past? No electricity, no mobile phones, no running water!

8. He studied **Ø** history at university.

9. Tim Berners-Lee invented **the** World Wide Web in the 1980s.

10. They try to recycle as much as possible as it's good for **the** environment.

11. What's **the** weather like in Australia at the moment?

12. I really like **the** climate here – not too hot, not too cold.

13. Celebrities often have a love/hate relationship with **the** press.

14. Most British people trust **the** police.

15. She learned **the** waltz at school.

16. I usually read **the** newspaper on Sundays.

17. The government is reducing the money it gives to **Ø** science.

18. I'll be in touch by **Ø** email.

19. We often go to **the** countryside for the weekend.

20. Please write your essay in **the** past tense.

Answers to Section 5

EXERCISE 5.1

1. I'm going to buy Julie **a** cake for her birthday.

2. I always go to **the** café around the corner from our house. You know the one.

3. Could you try to find me **a** new saucepan when you're at the shops?

4. What happened to the rest of **the** soup that we ate yesterday?

5. We'd like **a** large bottle of orange juice, please.

6. **The** water in my house is really brown!

7. Pass me **the** spoon next to your hand, please.

8. I'm looking for **a** job.

9. If I were you, I'd take **a** taxi to the airport.

10. Could you lend me **a** pen?

11. Do you know **a** good dentist?

12. Is there **a** park near here?

13. That child looks really cold. She needs **a** coat.

14. This is **the** plant that I told you about. Isn't it beautiful?

15. I wish I lived in **a** house by the sea.

EXERCISE 5.2

1. She's **a** lawyer.

2. That sounds like **a** lorry outside.

3. *Dr Seuss* is **a** children's book.

4. Maria and Juan are **Ø** engineers.

5. A Ferrari is a kind of **Ø** car.

6. Korma is **an** Indian dish.

7. Julia works as **a** waitress.

8. My nephew looked like **an** old man when he was born.

9. Basil is a variety of **Ø** herb.

10. A barrister is a sort of **Ø** lawyer.

11. That car is **a** Mercedes.

12. They are **Ø** very nice people.

13. Noriko and Kumiko are **Ø** students.

14. David is **a** professor.

15. What's in this box? It looks like **Ø** chocolate!

16. I work as **a** teacher.

17. That sounds like **a** bell.

18. Reggae is a kind of **Ø** music.

19. My sisters are **Ø** doctors.

20. Elizabeth is **an** extremely intelligent girl.

EXERCISE 5.3

1. What **a** cute baby!

2. What **Ø** fun!

3. What **Ø** heavy rain!

4. What **a** day!

5. What **Ø** fantastic music!

6. What **a** warm evening!

7. What **Ø** beautiful clothes!

8. What **a** horrible journey!

9. What **an** interesting book!

10. What **Ø** traffic!

EXERCISE 5.4

1. Lucy is **a** lawyer.

2. What **Ø** awful weather!

3. They looked like Ø thieves.

4. John and Susan are Ø Christians.

5. Does that farm sell Ø eggs?

6. This is a sort of Ø magazine.

7. What Ø delicious cakes!

8. She's looking for **a** Japanese teacher.

9. I need **a** cup of tea!

10. Could you pass me **a** glass?

11. Do you know **a** cheap restaurant near here?

12. We need Ø music!

13. Could you buy Ø pasta when you're at the shop?

14. Emma's at the market looking for Ø brown rice.

15. Are there Ø plants in your office?

16. This garden needs Ø grass!

17. What **a** lovely holiday!

18. Julie and Luke are Ø nurses.

19. I want Ø new cushions for my living room.

20. Do you have Ø lemonade?

EXERCISE 5.5

1. John works as **an** accountant.

2. What **an** ugly car!

3. What **a** tasty meal!

4. Several of my friends are Ø vegetarians.

5. What **a** fantastic prize!

6. What **Ø** interesting buildings!

7. I'd like to be **a** surgeon when I've finished university.

8. Espresso is a kind of **Ø** coffee.

9. That sounds like **Ø** water.

10. What **Ø** lovely food!

11. They advertised for **Ø** receptionists who know Spanish, German and Portuguese.

12. He'd like **Ø** new clothes.

13. She's **an** actress.

14. Yoshi and Yuka are **Ø** Buddhists.

15. That's a kind of **Ø** cake.

16. What **a** horrible story!

17. Richard's **a** taxi driver.

18. What **Ø** beautiful shoes!

19. My parents are **Ø** police officers.

20. I'd love **a** bigger house.

Answers to Section 6

EXERCISE 6.1

1. Could you tell me the answer to **Ø** question 6, please?

2. The trains from London arrive at **Ø** platform 7.

3. Her office is on **the** third floor.

4. John, could you read out **Ø** number three, please?

5. The description of the house is in **Ø** section eight of the book.

6. Could you pass me **the** first box on the right, please?

7. The diagram on **Ø** page 84 is not correct.

8. The classroom is on **the** second floor.

9. His flight leaves from **Ø** gate 18.

10. I don't know the answer to **the** eighth question.

11. The class will be held in **Ø** room 336.

12. We need to read **the** first part of the book for homework.

13. They live in **the** third flat.

14. The date of publication is normally on **the** first page of the book.

15. Please look at **Ø** diagram 23.

16. This is **the** first book I've ever read by this author.

17. Could you begin reading from the beginning of **Ø** part four?

18. They live in **Ø** flat 3.

19. Is this **the** first time that you've visited London?

20. She's **the** third person I've met this week who knows my sister!

EXERCISE 6.2

1. She was elected **Ø** president.

2. Catherine is **a** pilot.

3. I'm **a** bank clerk.

4. Adam is **Ø** CEO of our company.

5. Ellie was appointed **Ø** professor of philosophy at Oxford.

6. Mary was crowned **Ø** queen in 1543.

7. John works as **a** teacher.

8. Lucy's **a** lawyer.

9. He got a new job working as **a** shop assistant.

10. He became **Ø** treasurer in 2010.

EXERCISE 6.3

1. Can you speak Ø Turkish?

2. This book is written in Ø Arabic.

3. What's the answer to Ø question ten?

4. **The** winter that Julie was born was cold and snowy.

5. Would you like to have Ø dinner at home or shall we go out?

6. Have you ever tried Ø judo?

7. Did I tell you about **the** delicious lunch that we had in Paris?

8. Elizabeth was elected Ø President of the United States.

9. He's studying Ø Spanish.

10. The party is on **the** third of February.

11. I learned Ø tennis at school.

12. I had Ø breakfast in a café yesterday.

13. What are you doing at Ø Christmas?

14. Could you write Ø question number four on the board, please?

15. She speaks Ø English fluently.

16. He cooked **the** most amazing dinner.

17. Would you like to go to the cinema on Ø Friday night?

18. Ø Baseball is very popular in Japan.

19. Do you fast during Ø Ramadan?

20. Could you pass me **the** third book on the shelf, please?

EXERCISE 6.4

1. Do you remember **the** July when we met?

2. Shall we have coffee on Ø Monday?

3. Julie is studying Ø Japanese.

4. Could you come on **the** 6th of August?

5. The information about proper nouns is in Ø Section 9.

6. Do you play Ø rugby at school?

7. I love Ø summer!

8. She can speak Ø Spanish really well.

9. We often go on holiday in Ø May.

10. How about meeting on Ø Tuesday afternoon?

11. Please turn to Ø question D in your exam paper.

12. He was crowned Ø king in Westminster Abbey.

13. Ø Fact is, I don't like tea very much, even though I'm British.

14. Her office is on **the** second floor.

15. I love Ø skiing.

16. **The** winter that I was in Japan was one of the best winters of my life.

17. Do you celebrate Ø Easter?

18. The train leaves from Ø platform 6.

19. **The** English that they speak in Glasgow is quite different from how people speak in London.

20. He was elected Ø Prime Minister.

Answers to Section 7

EXERCISE 7.1

1. Look at **the** sky! It's a beautiful shade of pink!

2. Neil Armstrong explored in **a** moon buggy.

3. Have you had Ø lunch yet?

4. She can play **the** guitar really well.

5. I think we should fix the roof properly now, so we can avoid **Ø** future problems.

6. The government needs to think more about protecting **the** environment.

7. We had **a** Russian lesson every Friday when I was at university.

8. The children made a model of **the** world.

9. John has **a** cough.

10. The children can't leave the classroom until **the** lunch bell rings.

11. She bought **a** new work outfit.

12. They are learning to speak **Ø** Russian.

13. He's working as **a** guitar teacher.

14. Mary bought **Ø** cough medicine.

15. She loves **Ø** sky diving.

16. She's just graduated from university and is very excited about **the** future.

17. She works for **an** environment agency in Canada.

18. Did you see **the** moon last night? It was really bright.

19. They wished for **Ø** world peace.

20. He goes to **Ø** work on the train every day.

EXERCISE 7.2

1. The old actor died in **Ø** hospital last night.

2. She sometimes goes to **the** jail in our city as part of her job.

3. My son's studying history at **Ø** university.

4. When their houses were damaged in the storm, some people slept in **the** school nearby.

5. He spent three years in **Ø** prison.

6. Have you ever seen **the** university in Cambridge?

7. The lawyer stood up in **Ø** court and spoke to the jury.

8. **The** college in our city is very near the river.

9. Do your parents go to Ø church on Sundays?

10. Lucy is still at Ø school – she's only fourteen.

11. I won't break the law – I don't want to go to Ø jail!

12. My class visited **the** prison in our town last month – it was very interesting.

13. We'll meet outside **the** church at six.

14. The school children had a tour round **the** court near their school.

15. How many classes do you have at Ø college?

16. I went to **the** hospital today to see my friend who's a nurse.

EXERCISE 7.3

1. John is at Ø home now.

2. Let's go into Ø town later – I'd like to do some shopping.

3. I went to Ø bed early last night, but I still feel tired.

4. **The** work that Julie is doing at the moment sounds boring.

5. My son's just rented his first flat and needs furniture – I'm going to give him **the** bed in our spare room.

6. I usually arrive at Ø work at about eight thirty.

7. She bought a book about **the** homes of the rich and famous.

8. **The** town where my mother lives is very pretty.

EXERCISE 7.4

1. She has never had **the** measles.

2. Unfortunately, he was diagnosed with Ø cancer.

3. I felt ill, but I didn't have **a** temperature.

4. Her grandfather suffered from **Ø** heart disease.

5. Julie has **a** cold, so she's not coming swimming today.

6. John had **a** fever, and felt terrible.

7. He had **the** flu during the Christmas holidays.

8. I have such **a** headache. I think I'll go to bed early.

9. She had **a** cough all winter.

10. I very often get **the** hiccups.

EXERCISE 7.5

1. I don't like **the** AC at work. It's too cold.

2. Should we book **a** B&B or a hotel for our holiday?

3. She's studying **Ø** DNA at university.

4. Where is the headquarters of **Ø** NASA?

5. Do you know **the** ISBN of the book you want?

6. You should use a sun cream with **a** high SPF if you have fair skin.

7. There are a lot of stories about **Ø** UFOs. People find the idea of life on other planets interesting.

8. She's wanted to work for **the** BBC for a long time.

9. In the film, the hero is running away from **the** CIA.

10. Is there **an** ATM outside the station?

11. How many member states are there in **the** EU?

12. He worked as a reporter for **Ø** CNN.

13. The headquarters of **the** FBI is in Washington D.C.

14. There are thirty basketball clubs in **the** NBA.

15. He left **Ø** UNICEF some money in his will.

16. **The** UN sent aid to the country after the earthquake.

17. When does **the** WHO recommend weaning babies?

18. The website has **a** FAQ, but I couldn't find the information that I wanted there.

19. I need to call the bank and ask them to send me **a** new PIN.

20. Lord Ismay was the first Secretary General of **Ø** NATO.

EXERCISE 7.6

1. I have **a little** water left. There's enough to share.

2. I have **a few** good friends. I'm not lonely.

3. He has **little** education. He can't read or write, and he can hardly count.

4. There are **few** people she really trusts. It's a bit sad.

5. We've got **a little** time at the weekend. Would you like to meet?

6. Julie gave us **a few** apples from her garden. Shall we share them?

7. She has **little** self-confidence. She has a lot of trouble talking to new people.

8. There are **few** women politicians in the UK. There should be more.

9. It's a great pity, but this hospital has **little** medicine. They can't help many people.

10. I've got **a few** cakes to give away. Would you like one?

11. There's **a little** milk left in the fridge. It should be enough for our coffee.

12. **Few** children from this school go on to university, unfortunately.

13. Do you need information on English grammar? I have **a few** books on the topic if you would like to borrow them.

14. She's lucky. She has **few** problems.

15. The UK has **little** sunshine in the winter. That's why so many British people go on holiday to sunny places!

16. There's **a little** spaghetti left in the cupboard. Shall we eat it tonight?

17. There are **few** programmes on television that I want to watch. I prefer to download a film or read a book.

18. He has **little** free time. He hardly ever even manages to call his mother!

19. Unfortunately, I have **a few** problems at the moment.

20. Are you thirsty? There's **a little** juice left in this bottle, if you'd like it.

EXERCISE 7.7

1. She's **the most** beautiful girl that I've ever seen.

2. **Most** British people eat turkey at Christmas.

3. **Most** of the clothes in that shop are badly made.

4. I think that **the most** intelligent thing to do is to take a taxi.

5. He's **the most** interesting person I've spoken to today.

6. I think that **most** students will be very happy that the exams are finished.

7. **Most** of the cars on my street are black.

8. That is **the most** delicious cake that I've ever eaten!

9. The teacher told me that **most** of the children in her class like science.

10. I love living in London. I think it's **the most** exciting city in the world!

EXERCISE 7.8

1. Have you only got **one** brother? Jessie said you had three.

2. Only **one** of the students in my class passed the exam.

3. Could I have **a** cup of tea please.

4. I'd like **one** beer, not two.

5. There are at least **a** million people living in that city.

6. She's got **a** cat and **a** dog.

7. **One** of my friends was late but all the others were on time.

8. I'd like **a** large sandwich.

9. Julie's got **one** car, not seven!

10. There was **a** motorbike on the corner of the street.

11. Please give me **a** piece of paper.

12. He has **a** hundred pounds in his wallet.

13. He paid more than **a** thousand pounds for the ring.

14. He bought **one** of the TVs we looked at last week.

15. Can I have **one** of those doughnuts?

16. Can I have **a** glass of water?

17. Sorry, I only wanted **one** cup of coffee, not three!

18. She bought **a** car last week.

19. **One** of my friends lives in Shanghai.

20. **One** of these days I must clean out my garage.

EXERCISE 7.9

1. She's lived here for **a** year and a half.

2. She's lived here for **one** and a half years.

3. I bought **one** and a half kilos of tomatoes.

4. I bought **a** kilo and a half of tomatoes.

5. He was away for **a** week and a half.

6. He was away for **one** and a half weeks.

7. Luke walked **a** mile and a half to the party.

8. Luke walked **one** and a half miles to the party.

9. They arrived here **one** and a half months ago.

10. They arrived here **a** month and a half ago.

EXERCISE 7.10

1. I play football twice **a** week.

2. She calls her parents every **Ø** Sunday.

3. She's driving at 50 miles **an** hour.

4. The new train will go at 300 kilometres **an** hour.

5. The bananas cost £2 **a** kilo.

6. I meet my friend Julie every **Ø** week.

7. The water is 50 cents **a** litre.

8. We go out for dinner twice **a** month.

9. She goes to the gym three times **a** week.

10. I go on holiday to Spain every **Ø** year.

11. I work at the school a few days **a** month.

12. The ribbon cost £1 **a** metre.

13. He runs ten kilometres **a** day.

14. John has a meeting with his boss every **Ø** week.

15. The speed limit in London is 30 miles **an** hour.

16. Petrol is £1.50 **a** litre.

17. Lisa calls her grandfather twice **a** week.

18. I go to the library every **Ø** Saturday.

19. Those sandals are £10 **a** pair.

20. I visit my family every **Ø** year.

EXERCISE 7.11

1. I'm meeting Julie **Ø** next week.

2. We'll get on **the** next bus.

3. I arrived in New York Ø last month.

4. I can't believe he ate **the** last chocolate!

5. I'm going on holiday Ø next Friday.

6. She started college Ø last year.

7. I liked **the** last teacher. I don't think the new one is as good.

8. What are you doing Ø next month?

9. She asked directions from **the** next person she saw.

10. We didn't see John at all Ø last week.

11. Call me Ø next Tuesday.

12. I visited Kenya Ø last winter.

EXERCISE 7.12

1. Lucy came in Ø first place in the riding competition.

2. I won Ø second prize! Hurray!

3. Why don't I like living here? Ø First, it's too cold. Also, I miss my family.

4. I'd like **the** third cake on the shelf, please.

5. John went to the bank Ø first. Then he went to the library.

6. 'Which bottle do you want?' '**The** second one.'

7. She got on **the** first bus that came.

8. I've read **the** first book in the series, but I haven't read **the** second one.

9. 'How did Luke do in the race?' 'He came Ø third.'

10. Could you pass me **the** second cup on the right, please?

EXERCISE 7.13

1. I stayed in bed for a week when I had **the** / Ø flu.

2. I'll see you **Ø** next Tuesday.

3. I've got such **a** headache! Do you have any painkillers?

4. Fortunately, not many children get **the / Ø** measles nowadays.

5. She sees her family once **a** month.

6. **The** more it rains in London, **the** more I want a holiday!

7. There are **a** few biscuits left – would you like one?

8. She goes to the gym three times **a** week.

9. He usually watches the news on **the** BBC.

10. Could I just have **Ø** half a cup of coffee, please.

11. She donates money to **Ø** UNICEF every month

12. Jenny is **the** most intelligent student in the class.

13. John is at **the** hospital where he's visiting a friend.

14. The thief was sent to **Ø** jail for six years.

15. When I was at **Ø** university, none of the students had any money.

16. She gave **a** million pounds to charity.

17. Meet me **Ø** next week.

18. She arrives in New York **Ø** next month.

19. She has **Ø** few nice clothes, so she always looks scruffy.

20. I go to the cinema about twice **a** month.

EXERCISE 7.14

1. He has at least **a** hundred DVDs.

2. **The** more chocolate I eat, **the** happier I am!

3. He brushes his teeth twice **a** day.

4. I have **a** little money, so let's buy some ice cream.

5. She earns **a** thousand pounds a month.

6. We visited Canada **Ø** last year.

7. I went to **Ø** bed at nine o'clock last night.

8. He saw a photographer standing outside **the** court.

9. John used to work as a cleaner at **the** college.

10. **The** faster the car, **the** more he likes it.

11. The school children enjoyed going to **the** old jail.

12. They went to **Ø** court during their divorce proceedings.

13. I think **Ø** most people would like to have a bit more free time.

14. We meet twice or three times **a** year.

15. She has **Ø** little money, so she can't afford to heat her flat.

16. John's at **Ø** work at the moment.

17. She came to San Francisco **Ø** last December.

18. She's had **a** cold for three weeks.

19. Her grandfather had **Ø** heart disease.

20. Lucy's still at **Ø** school – she's studying for her exams at the moment.

EXERCISE 7.15

1. My grandmother goes to **Ø** church every week.

2. **The** church in my village is to be knocked down.

3. My hotel room didn't have **Ø** AC.

4. Could you pass me **the** third book on the right, please?

5. What's **the** most terrifying movie you've ever seen?

6. **Ø** Most animals in the UK are harmless.

7. She applied for a job at **the** university.

8. We went to **the** school to vote in the general election.

9. What are you studying at **Ø** college?

10. John had **a** temperature, so he went home.

11. She stayed in **Ø** hospital for a few days after she had her baby.

12. Let's go **Ø** home. I'm tired.

13. I need **a** new PIN.

14. I'd like to go into **Ø** town later. There are some things I'd like to buy.

15. I've recently started taking **Ø** piano lessons.

16. She bought **Ø** ballet shoes.

17. She works in **an** internet café.

18. Is there **a** football pitch near here?

19. **The** stronger the coffee, **the** better!

20. Emily won **Ø** first prize in the competition.

Answers to Section 8

EXERCISE 8.1

1. She bought some jewellery abroad, and sold it at **a** profit when she got home.

2. John's solution is correct to **a** certain extent. It will help, but it won't fix the problem completely.

3. I could see a mountain range in **the** distance.

4. I really like the museums in London, but I like the British Museum in **Ø** particular.

5. I love living in London on **the** whole (very occasionally it's difficult).

6. He seems nice normally, but behind **the** scenes he makes some deals I don't approve of.

7. He didn't realise he was in **Ø** danger from the tide until the coastguard arrived.

8. My brother was at **a** loose end at home, so he was pleased when his friend called.

9. Crime is on **the** increase. You should be careful of your bag.

10. I didn't break the vase on Ø purpose, Mummy! It was an accident.

11. David could tell at **a** glance that the news was bad.

12. I wanted to get some plums but I bought peaches by Ø mistake.

13. I called Julie on **the** off-chance that she was free for lunch.

14. That radio station reports the news in Ø brief at 7 a.m.

15. Our shower will be fixed next week. In **the** meantime, we can use the shower at the gym.

16. She thought she'd get better results if she studied harder, but, on **the** contrary, she needed to relax more instead.

17. I bought an old car with **a** view to fixing it up.

18. She crossed the room on Ø tiptoe, as the baby had just fallen asleep.

19. Julie is on **a** diet again! She's always trying to lose weight.

20. Are you in **the** habit of studying every day? If not, you need to start!

21. I made him a birthday cake in Ø secret.

22. The charity ball was for **a** good cause, so many people gave money.

23. I was in **a** hurry this morning and I forgot my umbrella.

24. Your wallet is in Ø front of the TV.

25. She likes her job in Ø general, but this week has been very stressful.

26. Please cut that piece of cake in Ø half. It's too much for one person!

27. Unfortunately, I don't see my old friends on **a** regular basis. We only meet rarely.

28. The doctor told him to stop smoking for **the** sake of his health.

29. In **a** sense, Rebecca is right. What she says is partly true.

30. I couldn't get to the door quickly because my suitcase was in **the** way.

31. If you don't get private tuition for the exam, you are at **a** disadvantage.

32. I usually drink tea, but today I thought I'd have coffee for **a** change.

33. It's difficult to study every day, but in **the** long run it will be worth it.

34. John loves living in the countryside. I, on **the** other hand, prefer the city.

35. I'm still in **Ø** touch with friends from school. We meet once a year.

36. Richard has been behaving very strangely recently. Perhaps he's in **Ø** love!

EXERCISE 8.2

1. This exercise is as easy as **Ø** pie.

2. My flat is absolutely tiny – there's no room to swing **a** cat.

3. It's no use crying over **Ø** spilt milk – the money is all gone.

4. I don't think Julie will come to the party tonight – she's feeling a bit under **the** weather.

5. It's difficult for them to make **Ø** ends meet.

6. Don't beat about **the** bush – say exactly what you think.

7. He often turned **a** blind eye to his employee's lateness, but today she went too far.

8. If his grandfather kicks **the** bucket, he'll be in trouble.

9. Let's call it **a** day. I'm tired and I'd like to go home.

10. My sister and I don't really see eye to **Ø** eye. We disagree on almost everything.

11. I got a letter from an old school friend out of **the** blue.

12. Don't make **a** mountain out of **a** molehill. The situation isn't as bad as you think.

13. They got engaged last week and plan to tie **the** knot next year.

14. She'll see him again when **Ø** pigs fly!

15. Please give me **a** hand with my homework. I don't know how to begin it.

EXERCISE 8.3

1. You're always at **a** loose end! Why don't you do something useful?

2. I think we should call it **a** day. I'm exhausted.

3. Even though I was in the middle of the city, I could see hills in **the** distance.

4. In Ø brief, what would you say the main problems are?

5. I try to save a little money every week. It'll be very useful in **the** long run.

6. I really hate mice and I hate mice in my house in Ø particular.

7. We usually go on holiday to Scotland, but this year we visited Paris for **a** change.

8. They only tied **the** knot last July, but they are already arguing.

9. Do you have meetings with your manager on **a** regular basis, or just now and then?

10. Obesity is on **the** increase, despite the best efforts of the government.

11. Learning English is as easy as Ø pie! No problem!

12. The young man met his girlfriend in Ø secret.

13. I don't always see Ø eye to eye with my boss, but he's okay.

14. The teacher turned **a** blind eye to his students leaving early on Friday afternoon. It was a lovely sunny day.

15. Dinner will be ready in an hour, but in **the** meantime, let's have a drink and some bread.

16. I felt at **a** disadvantage in the lecture, because all the other students had studied the material before.

17. I was feeling a bit under **the** weather, so I decided to go to bed early.

18. The little boy told his mother that he hadn't dropped the milk bottle on Ø purpose.

19. Could you please move your bicycle? It's in **the** way.

20. I couldn't reach the shelf, even on Ø tiptoe, so I had to get a ladder.

Answers to Section 9

EXERCISE 9.1

1. She travelled around Ø India last year.

2. I've never met anyone from Ø Chile.

3. We went on holiday to **the** Philippines.

4. Julie lived in Ø Japan for a year.

5. I wish we could visit Ø Spain.

6. Ø Turkey has some beautiful cities.

7. London is in **the** United Kingdom.

8. Did you visit Ø Mexico on your trip?

9. I'd love to go to **the** United States.

10. Have you ever been to Ø Colombia?

11. She comes from **the** UK.

12. I met a girl from Ø Mongolia last night.

13. How many times has John been to Ø China?

14. Last year he visited Ø New Zealand.

15. San Francisco is in **the** USA.

16. My brother lives in Ø Morocco.

17. I saw a television programme about Ø South Korea.

18. She went on holiday to Ø Russia.

19. I've never been to Ø Mexico.

20. Jan comes from **the** Netherlands.

EXERCISE 9.2

1. She has never been to Ø Lake Geneva.

2. They crossed **the** Sahara Desert by camel.

3. He flew across **the** Atlantic Ocean.

4. I've heard **the** Mekong is a very large river.

5. **The** Great Victoria Desert is in Australia.

6. Where is Ø Lake Titicaca?

7. Hawaii is in **the** Pacific Ocean.

8. He owns a house near Ø Lake Superior.

9. She lives near **the** river Thames.

10. We sailed around **the** Mediterranean.

11. **The** Kalahari Desert is in the south of Africa.

12. I'd love to visit **the** Red Sea.

13. Ø Lake Victoria is the largest lake in Africa.

14. Have you been to **the** Gobi Desert?

15. Her city is near **the** Yangtze River.

16. They went to an island in **the** Indian Ocean.

17. They went down **the** Amazon in a canoe.

18. People say that there is a monster in the bottom of Ø Loch Ness.

19. Is **the** Mississippi the longest river in the USA?

20. **The** Arabian Desert reaches from Egypt to Iran.

EXERCISE 9.3

1. Have you ever seen Ø Mount Fuji?

2. Brandon is from Ø California.

3. Ø Mount Cook is very beautiful.

4. He loves going to **the** Pyrenees.

5. Where did you stay in Ø Delhi?

6. My parents live in Ø New Jersey.

7. What's your favourite part of Ø London?

8. I've heard **the** Himalayas are very beautiful.

9. She lived in Ø New York for three years.

10. She visited **the** Andes.

11. He grew up near **the** Rocky Mountains in the USA.

12. She has a house in Ø Sussex.

13. Sydney is in Ø New South Wales.

14. Where is Ø Mount Ararat?

15. I've always wanted to visit Ø Tuscany.

16. We went to Ø Paris last July.

17. We went skiing in **the** Alps.

18. He had decided to climb Ø Everest.

19. Ø Mont Blanc is the highest mountain in Europe.

20. Ø Singapore is his favourite city.

EXERCISE 9.4

1. She really enjoys visiting Ø Asia.

2. My sister is living in Ø Argentina.

3. Ø Corsica is an island in the Mediterranean.

4. Ø New Zealand is really beautiful and green.

5. Would you like to visit **the** Bahamas?

6. Last year we went to Ø Sicily, an Italian island.

7. **The** Canary Islands are popular with tourists.

8. Have you ever been to **the** Azores?

9. Ø Baffin Island is part of Canada.

10. Cairo is the capital of Ø Egypt.

11. I have never been to Ø Africa.

12. Imagine living in Ø Antarctica!

13. Ø Hokkaido is an island in the north of Japan.

14. She travelled all over Ø South America.

15. Do you know where **the** Cook Islands are?

16. Have you ever been to Ø China?

17. How many countries are there in Ø Europe?

18. In Ø Australia there are quite a lot of snakes.

19. **The** Maldives are popular with honeymoon couples.

20. She visited Ø Long Island last summer.

EXERCISE 9.5

1. Have you visited **the** British Museum?

2. She stayed in **the** Savoy [hotel] when she was in London.

3. He studied at Ø Birkbeck College.

4. I've never been to **the** Royal Opera House.

5. We ate dinner in Ø Chinatown [area].

6. Ø St Paul's Cathedral is very beautiful.

7. She works in **the** Victoria and Albert Museum.

8. The play is on at Ø St Martin's Theatre.

9. I live in Ø Fulham [area].

10. **The** Globe [theatre] is near to the river.

11. Let's meet outside Ø Fulham Library.

12. We visited **the** University of Cambridge.

13. I love having dinner in Ø Claridge's [hotel].

14. Ø Stansted [airport] is quite far from the city.

15. She walked across Ø Hammersmith Bridge.

16. They stopped for a cocktail at **the** Dorchester [hotel].

17. She got married in Ø All Saints' Church.

18. **The** National Gallery is enormous.

19. I went to see the new film at **the** Odeon [cinema].

20. Maybe we can stay at Ø Brown's [hotel].

21. He studies at Ø Westminster School.

22. Ø Mayfair is an expensive part of London.

23. Ø Regent's Park is beautiful in the summer.

24. **The** Criterion [theatre] is in central London.

25. The train leaves from Ø Victoria [station].

26. I live near Ø Putney Bridge.

27. Ø Primark [shop] is very cheap.

28. I go to Ø King's Cross [station] to get the train to Scotland.

29. Let's go to Ø Hyde Park on Sunday.

30. She met me at Ø Gatwick [airport].

EXERCISE 9.6

1. He's so rich that he has **a** Van Gogh in his house.

2. When she was in the US, she met Barack Obama! **The** Barack Obama!

3. **A** Miss Smith called last night [I don't know Miss Smith].

4. Even though it's small, the museum has several Monets and **a** Rembrandt.

5. Could you please pick up Ø Mr Black at the airport? [We know Mr Black.]

6. Louise is a bit of **an** Einstein, isn't she? She always gets full marks on the tests.

7. We went on holiday with **the** Bells [Mr and Mrs Bell and their children].

8. My boss's name is Ø John Brown.

9. There's **a** Mr Jones here to see you [I don't know Mr Jones].

10. They had a dinner party and invited **the** Browns [Mr and Mrs Brown].

EXERCISE 9.7

1. I love the fountains in Ø Trafalgar Square.

2. They had a holiday by Ø Lake Geneva.

3. She went hiking in **the** Alps.

4. My son is studying at **the** University of Edinburgh.

5. She hiked near Ø Lake Titicaca.

6. Your son is **a** proper little Picasso! He's very good at drawing.

7. She loved **the** da Vinci that she saw in Paris, so she bought a print of it.

8. *A Tale of Two Cities* was written by Ø Charles Dickens.

9. We went to Ø Spain last year.

10. Ø Westminster Abbey is near to the Houses of Parliament.

11. She flew over **the** Sahara Desert.

12. Mount Cook is in Ø New Zealand.

13. She spent the winter in Ø Hokkaido, an island in Japan.

14. We can take the train to France from Ø St Pancras [station].

15. I love looking out across **the** Atlantic Ocean.

16. She grew up in Ø Africa.

17. Her plane lands at Ø Heathrow [airport].

18. **The** Thames is the river that runs through London.

19. I really love Ø Richmond Park.

20. We didn't stop near **the** Rocky Mountains when we were travelling.

21. Ø Oxford Street gets very busy at the weekends.

22. He saw **a** Michelangelo for the first time when he was in Italy.

23. There's a letter here from **a** Lucy Brown [I don't know Lucy Brown].

24. I've never eaten at **Ø** Nobu [restaurant].

25. Europeans often go on holiday near **the** Mediterranean.

EXERCISE 9.8

1. She visited **Ø** Peru last May.

2. **Ø** Tower Bridge looks amazing at night.

3. Julie would love to travel around **Ø** California.

4. **The** Canary Islands are part of Spain.

5. **The** National Theatre shows a lot of good plays.

6. They rented a house in **Ø** Tuscany for the summer.

7. We met her near **the** Prince Charles Cinema

8. I'd love to be able to stay at **the** Ritz [hotel]

9. I often drink coffee in **Ø** Starbucks

10. Have you been to **the** National Portrait Gallery yet?

11. I saw **Ø** Mount Fuji from the plane as I was leaving Tokyo.

12. Her cousin went to **Ø** London University.

13. Could you pass **the** Austen that's on the table, please?

14. He stayed with **the** Fords when he went to New York [Mr and Mrs Ford].

15. She stayed in **Ø** Taipei for two weeks.

16. We travelled around **Ø** Asia for our honeymoon.

17. We went shopping in **Ø** Harrods.

18. The town is close to **the** Great Victoria Desert.

19. **The** Science Museum is great for children.

20. There was an auction of **a** Caravaggio [painting].

21. Ø Helena called earlier. She left you a message.

22. Last night I was sitting next to David Beckham at the cinema. **The** David Beckham!

23. **The** Mississippi flows through New Orleans.

24. Have you ever been to Ø Rio de Janeiro?

25. She lives in **the** Bahamas.

Answers to Section 10

REVIEW EXERCISE 10.1

1. The cold winter has been difficult for **the** elderly. (Part 3.5)

2. My grandmother goes to Ø church twice a week. (Part 7.3)

3. John wants Ø new shoes. (Part 2.1.2)

4. I went to **the** supermarket that my mother suggested. (Part 2.4.1)

5. Give me **the** glass by the chair, please. (Part 2.4.2)

6. He spends all his time at **the** gym! (Part 4.1)

7. My boss and I almost always see eye to Ø eye. It's great to work with someone who has similar ideas. (Part 8.2)

8. I go to the hairdresser's twice **a** year. (Part 7.10)

9. We received Ø presents at Christmas. (Part 2.1.2)

10. She learned Ø English at school. (Part 6.1.1)

11. We often eat lamb on Ø Easter Sunday. (Part 6.2.3)

12. Do you call your mother on Ø Mother's Day? (Part 6.2.3)

13. Scotland is Ø coldest in January. (Part 2.4.5)

14. He studied at **the** University of London. (Part 9.3.3)

15. Let's meet on Ø Tuesday afternoon. (Part 6.2.5)

16. They always travelled by Ø car during their holiday. (Part 4.4)

17. The new railway line crosses the country from Ø east to Ø west. (Part 8.3)

18. Tourists usually visit **Ø** St Paul's Cathedral in London. (Part 9.3.1)

19. She loves seeing films at **the** Prince Charles Cinema. (Part 9.3.3)

20. What **a** lovely necklace! (Part 5.3)

REVIEW EXERCISE 10.2

1. We went to **Ø** Sicily last year. (Part 9.2.1)

2. I saw them walking **Ø** arm in **Ø** arm. (Part 8.3)

3. He won a prize for dancing **the** tango. (Part 4.9)

4. The government is trying to lower **Ø** unemployment. (Part 4.15)

5. Lucy had **a** headache and went to bed early. (Part 7.5)

6. I've never been to **Ø** Bali [an island in Indonesia]. (Part 9.2.1)

7. **The** Nile is the longest river in the world. (Part 9.2.2)

8. In New York, many people jog in **Ø** Central Park. (Part 9.3.1)

9. She bought **a** new handbag. (Part 2.1.2)

10. I had **the / Ø** flu last year and was off work for two weeks. (Part 7.5)

11. I had **a** piece of cake and **a** cup of coffee. (Part 2.1.2)

12. A sloe is a kind of **Ø** fruit. (Part 5.2)

13. Do you know much about **the** history of India? (Part 3.2.1)

14. He writes about **the** rich and famous for a magazine. (Part 3.5)

15. She gave me **the** last chocolate. (Part 2.4.4)

16. I've read **the** book that our professor lent me. (Part 2.4.1)

17. She ate **the** cakes that her brother had made. (Part 2.4.1)

18. She has **Ø** few books – she wishes she could afford more. (Part 7.7)

19. Could you lend me **a** pen? (Part 5.1.2)

20. Leonardo da Vinci died in **the** sixteenth century. (Part 6.2.7)

REVIEW EXERCISE 10.3

1. I'd like to go to a restaurant for **a** change. We always eat at home these days. (Part 8.1)

2. **The** more you study, **the** better your exam result will be. (Part 7.13)

3. She likes to stop for a coffee on the way to work in **the** morning. (Part 4.12)

4. He got **the / Ø** hiccups and they lasted all afternoon. (Part 7.5)

5. I'm interested in **the** history of Africa. (Part 3.2.1)

6. Have you flown across **the** Pacific? (Part 9.2.2)

7. She loves **Ø** fourteenth-century art. (Part 3.2.1)

8. I love **Ø** cheese. (Part 3.1)

9. I've never been to **Ø** Portugal. (Part 9.2.1)

10. I thought she was going to come early but, on **the** contrary, she's already thirty minutes late. (Part 8.1)

11. After class, Lucy went **Ø** home and called her boyfriend. (Part 7.4.2)

12. **The** Swiss make great chocolate. (Part 3.6)

13. We saw that film **Ø** last month. (Part 7.11)

14. There's **a** fantastic restaurant near her flat. (Part 2.7)

15. I arrived in Mexico in **Ø** April. (Part 6.2.1)

16. We had sandwiches and Coke for lunch. **The** Coke was warm, though. (Part 2.5)

17. We met at **Ø** Victoria Station. (Part 9.3.1)

18. I need **a** cup of tea! (Part 5.1.2)

19. I'm feeling a bit under **the** weather, so I don't think I'll come to the party tonight. (Part 8.2)

20. It costs **a** hundred pounds. (Part 7.9.1)

REVIEW EXERCISE 10.4

1. Julie is **a** teacher. (Part 5.2)

2. What will life be like in **the** twenty-second century? (Part 6.2.7)

3. Could I use **the** internet at your place? (Part 4.14)

4. I want to talk to him **Ø** face to **Ø** face. (Part 8.3)

5. My daughter is still at **Ø** school – she's only fifteen. (Part 7.3)

6. She hates **Ø** mushrooms. (Part 3.1)

7. Lucy bought **the** dress that you recommended. (Part 2.4.1)

8. I'll take the exam again **Ø** next spring. (Part 7.11)

9. **Ø / The** problem is, the weather will be really cold in December. (Part 6.6)

10. English articles are as easy as **Ø** pie! I haven't made any mistakes with this exercise. (Part 8.2)

11. **The** hotter the curry, **the** more Richard eats! (Part 7.13)

12. Have you ever tried playing **Ø** rugby? (Part 6.1.3)

13. They are **Ø** Muslims. (Part 5.2)

14. Do you like **Ø** French cheese? (Part 3.2.1)

15. I travel around London by **Ø** underground. (Part 4.4)

16. I went to a party on **Ø** New Year's Eve. (Part 6.2.3)

17. Let's go out tonight – I'd love to see a play at **the** National Theatre. (Part 9.3.2)

18. **Ø** Big lorries are very noisy and can damage the roads. (Part 3.2.1)

19. I'm going to my yoga class on **Ø** Thursday morning. (Part 6.2.5)

20. I often go to **the** park during the summer. (Part 4.1)

REVIEW EXERCISE 10.5

1. My mother often goes to **the** Canary Islands on holiday. (Part 9.2.2)

2. They are all **Ø** very good students. (Part 5.2)

3. **Ø** Scotch beef is very popular here. (Part 3.2.1)

4. I don't know exactly when I'll finish my course – but sometime in **the** next year. (Part 7.11)

5. Do you speak Ø Spanish? (Part 6.1.1)

6. He drank Ø water. (Part 2.1.2)

7. She's studying Ø music at college. (Part 4.15)

8. We wrote an essay about **the** environment. (Part 4.14)

9. Ø Children should go to school. (Part 3.1)

10. I wrote her address on **the** back of an envelope. (Part 2.4.3)

11. Let's go into Ø town this afternoon and go to the cinema. (Part 7.4.4)

12. I watched Ø CNN all night. (Part 7.6.1)

13. There's **a** wallet on the grass. (Part 2.1.2)

14. Who would like to try Ø question 10? (Part 6.3)

15. Do you do anything special on Ø Christmas Eve? (Part 6.2.3)

16. **The** wind howled round the house all night. (Part 4.11)

17. We have Ø little in the fridge – I think we should go out for dinner. (Part 7.7)

18. There is a good café near **the** jail. (Part 7.3)

19. **The** university in Cambridge is very beautiful. (Part 7.3)

20. We meet for coffee twice **a** week. (Part 7.10)

REVIEW EXERCISE 10.6

1. My flat is absolutely tiny – there's no room to swing **a** cat. (Part 8.2)

2. We met in **a** café. (Part 2.1.2)

3. She became Ø queen in 1952. (Part 6.5)

4. What do you think of Ø life abroad? (Part 4.15)

5. Ø Lions are very dangerous. (Part 3.1)

6. Ø Flamingos are pink and white. (Part 3.1)

7. Ø Mount Fuji is a very beautiful mountain. (Part 9.2.1)

8. Richmond Park is **the** biggest park in London. (Part 2.4.5)

9. He was elected Ø president last year. (Part 6.5)

10. He's very keen on Ø baseball. (Part 6.1.3)

11. She's interested in **the** music of the 1970s. (Part 3.2.1)

12. Her birthday is Ø July 21st. (Part 6.2.4)

13. What would you like for Ø lunch? (Part 6.1.2)

14. Which is **the** biggest city in the world? (Part 2.4.5)

15. John and Lucy finally tied **the** knot last week and they're going on honeymoon to Mexico tomorrow. (Part 8.2)

16. Amanda's **a** doctor. (Part 5.2)

17. What are you doing at **the** weekend? Would you like to have lunch? (Part 4.12)

18. What Ø cold water! (Part 5.3)

19. My brother was born in **the** 1980s. (Part 6.2.7)

20. **The** bigger the cake, **the** better I like it! (Part 7.13)

REVIEW EXERCISE 10.7

1. I went to the train station early on Ø purpose. I knew it would be very busy. (Part 8.1)

2. The thief is in Ø court today. (Part 7.3)

3. I've never been keen on Ø dogs. (Part 3.1)

4. Ø Lions hunt in groups. (Part 3.1)

5. Sorry, that's **the** wrong answer. (Part 2.4.4)

6. She often gives money to **the** homeless. (Part 3.5)

7. We need to learn about **the** history of China. (Part 3.2.1)

8. She's interested in Ø animals. (Part 3.1)

9. Could you look for **a** large rug at the shops? (Part 5.1.2)

10. I loved Ø Barcelona. (Part 9.2.1)

11. When I was a child, we always dressed up for Ø Halloween. (Part 6.2.3)

12. They climbed part of the way up Ø Everest. (Part 9.2.1)

13. At 1 a.m. she finally called it **a** day, and went to bed. (Part 8.2)

14. She sent the bill by Ø email. (Part 4.5)

15. On **the** whole, I like travelling, even if occasionally it can get a bit lonely. (Part 8.1)

16. Please turn to Ø section 7 of your exam paper. (Part 6.3)

17. I want to buy **a** big house near the river. Do you know of any that are for sale? (Part 5.1.2)

18. She has a shower once **a** day. (Part 7.10)

19. What's the answer to Ø question 5? (Part 6.3)

20. The North Pole is in **the** Arctic. (Part 9.2.1)

REVIEW EXERCISE 10.8

1. I like going to **the** mountains on holiday, but my husband prefers **the** beach. (Part 4.10)

2. He's reading about Ø NATO. (Part 7.6.2)

3. I kept in Ø touch with my classmates for years after we met. (Part 8.1)

4. Julie and Lucy are Ø very nice girls. (Part 5.2)

5. We had dinner in a restaurant last night. **The** waitress was very friendly. (Part 2.6)

6. I went to a hotel on holiday and I really enjoyed swimming in **the** pool. (Part 2.6)

7. What **a** fantastic party! (Part 5.3)

8. He sat down on **the** chair and put his feet on **the** stool [there's one chair and one stool near us] (Part 2.2)

9. What language do Ø / **the** Lithuanians speak? (Part 3.6)

10. They went to **the** Himalayas. (Part 9.2.2)

11. What Ø spicy food! (Part 5.3)

12. I'm so tired, I'd like to go to **Ø** bed – even though it's only lunchtime! (Part 7.4.1)

13. She took **the / a** plane to Paris. (Part 4.4)

14. Do you know **an** accountant? I need help with my tax forms! (Part 5.1.2)

15. Can you play **Ø** golf? (Part 6.1.3)

16. Did he really use to work for **the** FBI? (Part 7.6.1)

17. Is this garden open to **the** public? (Part 4.14)

18. She's going on **a** world tour. I'm so jealous! (Part 7.1)

19. **The** station is near the park [the station in our town]. (Part 2.3)

20. Is there **a** French speaker at your work? I need someone to translate this document. (Part 5.1.2)

REVIEW EXERCISE 10.9

1. I need **a** new car! My old one is about to fall apart. (Part 5.1.2)

2. London is **Ø** best in the summer. (Part 2.4.5)

3. **Ø** Sugar is bad for your health. (Part 3.1)

4. That's **the** only book I own. (Part 2.4.4)

5. **Ø / The** Moroccans speak French and Arabic. (Part 3.6)

6. I'm interested in **the** music of Ireland. (Part 3.2.1)

7. The government is trying to improve education for **the** young. (Part 3.5)

8. What's **the** price of a cup of coffee in Moscow? (Part 2.4.3)

9. She went out for dinner with her husband on **Ø** Valentine's Day. (Part 6.2.3)

10. We went to **Ø** Chelsea [an area of London] and had breakfast in a lovely café. (Part 9.3.1)

11. I dropped a cup and a glass. **The** glass smashed. (Part 2.5)

12. John's **a** vegetarian. (Part 5.2)

13. There was a sofa in **the** middle of the floor. (Part 2.4.3)

14. David's **a** professor. (Part 5.2)

15. I had **a** cold and couldn't go to work for a week. (Part 7.5)

16. She loves **Ø** nature and being outside. (Part 4.15)

17. I had **a** piano lesson this morning. (Part 7.1)

18. What do Jewish people do during **Ø** Passover? (Part 6.2.3)

19. They celebrate **Ø** Chinese New Year. (Part 6.2.3)

20. I love looking at **the** moon on a clear night. (Part 2.3)

REVIEW EXERCISE 10.10

1. She only wears **Ø** red shoes. (Part 3.2.1)

2. I usually take **the / a** train to Scotland. (Part 4.4)

3. She bought **Ø** rice and **Ø** vegetables. (Part 2.1.2)

4. **Ø / The** Colombians tend to like socialising. (Part 3.6)

5. I love reading **Ø** Spanish poetry. (Part 3.2.1)

6. They speak **Ø** French very well indeed. (Part 6.1.1)

7. Could you move your luggage please? It's in **the** way. (Part 8.1)

8. He's **an** architect. (Part 5.2)

9. Please close **the** window [there's only one open in the room]. (Part 2.2)

10. **The** poor sometimes don't have good access to education. (Part 3.5)

11. My plane arrives at **Ø** Heathrow [airport] about 6 a.m. (Part 9.3.1)

12. She's from **the** UK. (Part 9.2.1)

13. His birthday is in **Ø** October. (Part 6.2.1)

14. It's lovely to have **Ø** trees in cities. (Part 3.1)

15. Do you prefer **the** city or **the** country? (Part 4.10)

16. He's studying **Ø** Hindi. (Part 6.1.1)

17. He loves **the** music of Africa. (Part 3.2.1)

18. I went to Scotland at **Ø** Christmas. (Part 6.2.3)

19. My brother's **a** surgeon. (Part 5.2)

20. Lucy is **the** cleverest girl I know. (Part 2.4.5)

REVIEW EXERCISE 10.11

1. Let's meet in **the** café next to the station. (Part 2.4.2)

2. What **Ø** delicious pasta! (Part 5.3)

3. She's going to visit Budapest **Ø** next week. (Part 7.11)

4. There's **a** nice café in my hometown. (Part 2.7)

5. I have **the** same dress as you. (Part 2.4.4)

6. She goes to **the** cinema every month (Part 4.1)

7. We had a cup of coffee in **the** cafeteria at university [there's only one cafeteria there so the listener knows which one I mean]. (Part 2.3)

8. She studied **the** history of Europe. (Part 3.2.1)

9. The plane leaves from **Ø** gate 25. (Part 6.3)

10. We went to **the** theatre all the time when we were students (Part 4.1)

11. Do you ever go to **the** zoo? I love the penguins! (Part 4.1)

12. What **a** beautiful garden! (Part 5.3)

13. Lucy works as **a** hairdresser. (Part 5.2)

14. **The** college is on King Street. (Part 7.3)

15. Hand me **the** knives and forks, please [the knives and forks on the table]. (Part 2.2)

16. This new centre is a place where **the** unemployed can come for help and support. (Part 3.5)

17. She went shopping on **Ø** Oxford Street, but it was very busy. (Part 9.3.1)

18. **Ø** Kittens drink milk. (Part 3.1)

19. My son David had **a** temperature, so we took him to the doctor. (Part 7.5)

20. Do you like Ø athletics? (Part 6.1.3)

REVIEW EXERCISE 10.12

1. Could you come on **the** 31st of October? (Part 6.2.4)

2. Gordon can play **the** piano really well. (Part 4.3)

3. She went to school on Ø foot. (Part 4.4)

4. Can anyone play **the** guitar? (Part 4.3)

5. My parents are Ø accountants. (Part 5.2)

6. Does she visit her family during Ø Ramadan? (Part 6.2.3)

7. Have you read **the** newspaper this morning? (Part 4.5)

8. Their house is by **the** Indian Ocean. (Part 9.2.2)

9. I bought three plants and some pots at the garden centre. I put **the** plants in my garden. (Part 2.5)

10. Do you drink Ø coffee? (Part 3.1)

11. I'd like **a** cup of tea. (Part 5.1.2)

12. I went to Scotland Ø last Christmas. (Part 7.11)

13. Do you have Ø internet access at home? (Part 7.1)

14. There's a test at **the** end of the course. (Part 2.4.3)

15. My favourite month is Ø May. (Part 6.2.1)

16. She buys her stamps from **the** post office. (Part 4.2)

17. He got a new laptop and a phone last year. **The** phone has already broken. (Part 2.5)

18. We ordered lunch in a café. **The** sandwiches were delicious. (Part 2.6)

19. I bought a new bicycle last week. **The** wheels are red. (Part 2.6)

20. There's **a** beautiful dress in that shop. (Part 2.7)

REVIEW EXERCISE 10.13

1. There are at least **a** million people living there. (Part 7.9.1)

2. **Ø** Penguins live in cold places. (Part 3.1)

3. He got married on **the** 5th of April. (Part 6.2.4)

4. She's from **Ø** Bogotá. (Part 9.2.1)

5. I'm **a** student. (Part 5.2)

6. **Ø** Swans have babies called cygnets. (Part 3.1)

7. The adverts were sent by **Ø** post. (Part 4.5)

8. That sounds like **a** tractor! (Part 5.2)

9. She loves playing **Ø** tennis. (Part 6.1.3)

10. This is **the** coldest winter in a long time. (Part 2.4.5)

11. It must have been amazing to be an artist in Italy during **the** Renaissance. (Part 6.2.7)

12. Shall we meet on **Ø** Tuesday? (Part 6.2.2)

13. He studies **Ø** German philosophy. (Part 3.2.1)

14. I often fall asleep on **the** bus and miss my stop. (Part 4.4)

15. I like reading **Ø** Russian novels. (Part 3.2.1)

16. **Ø / The** fact is, I don't really like chocolate. (Part 6.6)

17. Lucy is often on **the** phone. (Part 4.5)

18. I'm **Ø** happiest when I'm sitting in the sunshine. (Part 2.4.5)

19. He went to **the** hospital to visit his friend. (Part 7.3)

20. London is **an** exciting city. (Part 5.2)

REVIEW EXERCISE 10.14

1. **The** British don't seem to mind the weather in the UK. (Part 3.6)

2. She did her master's degree at Ø Cambridge University. (Part 9.3.3)

3. She has **a** few books – they look good on the shelf. (Part 7.7)

4. I had toast and coffee for Ø breakfast today. (Part 6.1.2)

5. The speed limit is 30 miles **an** hour. (Part 7.10)

6. Lucy was in such **a** hurry she forgot to lock the door. (Part 8.1)

7. Julie can speak Ø Japanese fluently. (Part 6.1.1)

8. Do you know if there's **a** good café near here? (Part 5.1.2)

9. She loves having coffee outside in **the** sunshine. (Part 4.11)

10. I don't like travelling at Ø night. (Part 4.12)

11. A solicitor is a kind of Ø lawyer. (Part 5.2)

12. You can open an account at **the / a** bank. (Part 4.2)

13. She had **a** cough all winter. (Part 7.5)

14. Could you write the answer to Ø number 8 on the board please? (Part 6.3)

15. Shall we have Ø dinner at eight? (Part 6.1.2)

16. Is there **a** FAQ on the website? (Part 7.6.2)

17. Let's have a cup of coffee in Ø Starbucks. (Part 9.3.3)

18. I could see at **a** glance that the flat had been burgled. (Part 8.1)

19. The train on Ø platform 4 is for London. (Part 6.3)

20. That film is **a** comedy. (Part 5.2)

REVIEW EXERCISE 10.15

1. She was an interpreter for the UN. (Part 7.6.1)

2. She learned to play the flute when she was at school. (Part 4.3)

3. The book will be published in Ø September. (Part 6.2.1)

4. Pass me the book on the floor. (Part 2.4.2)

5. She had the / Ø measles when she was a child. (Part 7.5)

6. He played the saxophone in a band. (Part 4.3)

7. She picked up the wrong coat by Ø mistake. (Part 8.1)

8. His house is near the Thames [the river in London]. (Part 9.2.2)

9. We travelled around Ø South America for six months. (Part 9.2.1)

10. We had afternoon tea at the Dorchester [a hotel]. (Part 9.3.2)

11. School children in London often go to the British Museum. (Part 9.3.2)

12. I listened to the tennis match on the radio. (Part 4.5)

13. She spent two weeks travelling around Ø Tuscany [a region in Italy]. (Part 9.2.1)

14. She looks like a gymnast. (Part 5.2)

15. We sat by the fire and listened to the rain. (Part 4.11)

16. I'm looking for a pair of small, black shoes. I'm going to go shopping tomorrow. (Part 5.1.2)

17. There's a little milk left – enough for our coffee. (Part 7.7)

18. She was appointed Ø CEO in March. (Part 6.5)

19. I usually arrive at Ø work about nine in the morning. (Part 7.4.3)

20. Ø Cats like chasing Ø mice. (Part 3.1)

Answers to Appendices

APPENDIX EXERCISE A1.1

1. **An** Easter egg

2. **A** European holiday

3. **An** umbrella

4. **A** yellow dress

5. **A** car

6. **A** beautiful view

7. **An** hour

8. **A** uniform

9. **An** orange

10. **An** interesting day

11. **A** sofa

12. **An** ugly picture

'A' AND 'THE' EXPLAINED • 227

13. **An** expensive suit

14. **A** clever student

15. **A** university library

16. **A** child

17. **A** good teacher

18. **An** original idea

19. **A** park

20. **A** useful book

APPENDIX EXERCISE A1.2

1. The teacher wrote **an** 'A' on the student's work.

2. You can print **a** PDF.

3. She got **an** iPod for her birthday.

4. My brother drives **a** BMW.

5. Her name is Gillian with **a** G.

6. She has **an** IQ of 160.

7. The lecturer gave the student **an** 'F'.

8. I bought **a** CD.

9. He thought he saw **a** UFO.

10. There's **an** ATM round the corner.

APPENDIX EXERCISE A2.1

1. Mrs Brown   b: proper noun

2. Library   a: common noun

3. London   b: proper noun

4. Dog   a: common noun

5. Chicago   b: proper noun

6. Spain   b: proper noun

7. Houses   a: common noun

8. Nile	b: proper noun	
9. Chair	a: common noun	
10. Money	a: common noun	

APPENDIX EXERCISE A2.2

1. book	a: singular countable
2. countries	b: plural countable
3. T-shirts	b: plural countable
4. fridge	a: singular countable
5. laptops	b: plural countable
6. water	c: uncountable
7. computers	b: plural countable
8. universes	b: plural countable
9. plates	b: plural countable
10. love	c: uncountable
11. rice	c: uncountable
12. cup	a: singular countable
13. apple	a: singular countable
14. toothbrushes	b: plural countable
15. shoe	a: singular countable
16. tea	c: uncountable
17. train	a: singular countable
18. phones	b: plural countable
19. paint	c: uncountable
20. spaghetti	c: uncountable

21. handbag	a: singular countable	
22. steaks	b: plural countable	
23. toothpaste	c: uncountable	
24. ring	a: singular countable	
25. research	c: uncountable	
26. weather	c: uncountable	
27. watch	a: singular countable	
28. chairs	b: plural countable	
29. furniture	c: uncountable	
30. dust	c: uncountable	

APPENDIX EXERCISE A2.3

1. We have a lot of **homework**.

2. She does **research** at the university.

3. I need Ø knowledge about history.

4. He had a lot of fun at the party. [Correct]

5. We need some new **furniture**.

6. How **much baggage** do you have?

7. I need more **information**.

8. I hope we have Ø good weather on holiday.

9. We made Ø progress with the work.

10. Do you have any cash? [Correct]

11. The news **is** good.

12. I need Ø accommodation for tonight.

13. Can we have **spaghetti** for dinner?

14. There was Ø snow last night.

15. Hope you have Ø good luck!

APPENDIX EXERCISE A2.4

1. That actress has lovely **hair**.

2. The government is trying to encourage business by reducing taxes. [Correct]

3. She bought four cheeses. [Correct]

4. I eat **chicken** and chips very often.

5. The news is very bad, I'm afraid. [Correct]

6. The planes make a lot of **noise**.

6. The lecturer gave **a** talk about art history.

8. She ordered two mineral waters. [Correct]

9. There were lambs playing in the field. [Correct]

10. My garden gets a lot of **light**.

APPENDIX EXERCISE A2.5

1. She bought me a tea and a slice of cake. [Correct]

2. You can leave your **luggage** here.

3. We don't eat **much** rice at home.

4. I'm looking for Ø information about hotels.

5. She had a huge selection of different teas. [Correct]

6. Could I have a coffee? [Correct]

7. Could you give me Ø / **some** advice?

8. I need Ø assistance with this.

9. She appreciates beauty. [Correct]

10. Have you done your **homework**?

11. The traffic **was** terrible this morning.

12. We haven't made much progress, I'm afraid. [Correct]

13. She ate yogurt with blueberries. [Correct]

14. She bought carrots and **spinach**.

15. There is a lot of **research** into this problem.

16. The money **is** on the table.

17. There isn't much evidence against the person accused of the crime. [Correct]

18. Do you have Ø work?

19. Ø Fun is important, but don't forget to study too.

20. Experience is often more important than qualifications. [Correct]

APPENDIX EXERCISE A3.1

1. Can you buy **some** pasta? [I'm thinking of the amount we need for tonight.]

2. We need Ø mushrooms [I'm not thinking about the amount].

3. John drinks Ø coffee every morning [coffee, not tea].

4. Add **some** water to the soup if it's too thick [a certain amount of water].

5. I really want **some** tea – could you get me a cup?

6. We could have Ø rice for dinner [rice, not pasta].

7. I ate **some** bread and two eggs for lunch [I'm thinking about the amount].

8. She bought **some** new furniture [a certain amount of furniture].

9. Did you get Ø carrots? [I'm not thinking about the amount.]

10. I'd like Ø tea, please! [Tea, not juice or coffee.]

APPENDIX EXERCISE A3.2

1. Have we got **any** bread? [A real question, I have no idea.]

2. **Any** student will tell you that they don't have enough money [it doesn't matter which student].

3. We've got **some** furniture, but we still need a table.

4. She bought **some** new clothes.

5. You can buy beer in **any** pub [it doesn't matter which pub].

6. Can I have **some** more juice? [I expect you will say 'yes'.]

7. Did you buy **any** juice? [I have no idea, this is a real question.]

8. I can speak **some** French.

9. Would you like **some** tea? [An offer – I think you will say 'yes'.]

10. In London in the winter there's hardly **any** sunlight.

11. Go into **any** shop on the high street and ask [it doesn't matter which shop].

12. Would you like **some** more meat? [An offer – I think you will say 'yes'.]

13. There's **some** money in my handbag.

14. Did you buy **some** chicken? [I expect you will say 'yes' because we talked about it before.]

15. I don't have **any** sunblock with me.

16. She never drinks **any** water.

17. Do you have **some** sugar? [I expect you will say 'yes', because usually you have sugar.]

18. It's hard in a new city without **any** friends.

19. I didn't find **any** problems.

20. Could you give me **some** paper? [A request – I expect you will say 'yes'.]

Index

a few, 96
a little, 96
a lot, 97
acronyms, 94
adjectives, 19
advice, 85
afternoon, 52
air, 15
airport, 45, 124
anger, 84
areas in a city, 123
art, 54
art galleries, 125
back of, 18
baker's, 44
ballet, 43
bank, 44
bays, 119
beach, 50
beauty, 156
bed, 89
beginning of, 18
bike, 46
boat, 45
bottom of, 18
breakfast, 71
bridges, 124
bus, 45
bus station, 45
bus stop, 45
business, 155
cake, 156
calm, 84
cancer, 92
car, 46
centuries, 74
chicken, 155
chill, 92
church, 87
churches, 124

cinema, 43
cities, 119
city, 50
class, 87
classifying, 64
climate, 53
climate change, 54
cloth, 156
cold (illness), 92
college, 88
colleges, 125
communication and media, 47
comparatives, 107
continents, 118
cough, 92
countries, 118
countryside, 50
courage, 84
court, 88
crime, 54
dances, 50
dates, 73
day, 52
days of the week, 73
daytime, 52
deaf, 36
decades, 74
dentist's, 44
deserts, 120
dinner, 71
disabled, 36
doctor's, 44
edge of, 18
education, 85
elderly, 36
email, 47
end of, 18
entertainment and recreation, 43
enthusiasm, 84
environment, 53

233

ethical beliefs, 65
evening, 52
evil, 84
example of, 66
exclamations, 67
experience, 156
fact is, 79
ferry, 45
fever, 92
fire brigade, 53
first, 106
fixed expressions, 111
flu, 91
fog, 51
foxtrot, 50
fractions, 99
friendship, 84
front of, 18
fun, 85
furniture, 86
future, 53
future perfect tense, 53
general knowledge, 14
geographical expressions, 50
geographical names, 118
global warming, 54
government, 14
grammatical expressions, 53
gym, 43
hair, 155
hairdresser's, 44
half, 101
harm, 84
headache, 92
health, 85
heart disease, 92
height of, 18
help, 85
hiccups, 91
historical periods, 75
history, 54
holidays and special days, 73
home, 90
homeless, 36
homework, 86

hospital, 88
hotels, 125
hungry, 36
idioms, 113
illnesses, 91
information, 85
institutions, 87
intelligence, 84
internet, 53
inventions, 48
islands, 119
islands (in groups), 120
jail, 88
jewellery, 86
jobs, 65, 78
joy, 84
kind of, 66
knowledge, 84
lakes, 118
lamb, 156
languages, 71, 72
larger situation, 14
last, 19, 104
length of, 18
letters, 75
library, 44
life, 54
light, 156
literature, 54
look like, 65
lots, 97
love, 84
luck, 54, 85
luggage, 86
lunch, 71
mail, 47
meals, 71, 72
measles, 91
melancholy, 84
metro, 45
middle of, 18
money, 86
months, 73
moon, 15, 141
morning, 52

most, 98
motorbike, 46
mountain ranges, 120
mountains, 50, 118
museums, 125
music, 54
musical instruments, 44, 82
nationalities, 37
nature, 54
news, 85
newspaper, 155, 223
newspaper headlines, 77
newspapers, 47
next, 19, 104
night, 52
noise, 155
noun adjuncts, 82
numbers, 75, 99
oceans, 120
of-phrases, 18
old, 36
on foot, 46
one, 99
only, 19
opera, 43
ordinal numbers, 106
paper, 155
parallel structures, 115
park, 43
parks, 123
parts of the body, 48
parts of the day, 74
past, 53
past tense, 53
patience, 84
peace, 85
philosophy, 54
places in a city, 123
plane, 45
planets, 15
police, 53
political beliefs, 65
pollution, 54
poor, 36
possessive, 20

post, 47
post office, 44
post-modification, 32
poverty, 54
powerful, 36
pre-modification, 32
prepositional phrases, 17, 111
present, 53
present simple tense, 53
press, 53
price of, 18
prison, 88
problem is, 79
progress, 85
proper nouns, 118
provinces, 119
pub, 44
public, 53
pubs, 125
Queen, 14
question is, 79
radio, 47
rain, 51
regions, 119
relative clauses, 16
religious beliefs, 65
rich, 36
right, 19
rivers, 120
roads, 124
same, 19
school, 88
schools, 125
science, 54
sea, 50
seas, 120
seaside, 50
seasons, 74
second, 106
serenity, 85
shops, 124
shops and other businesses, 44
silence, 85
size of, 18
sky, 15

snow, 51
society, 54
solar system, 15
sort of, 66
sound, 156
sound like, 65
space, 54
sports, 71, 72
squares, 124
stars, 15
states, 119
station, 45
stations, 124
streets, 124
subway, 45
sun, 15, 86
sunshine, 51
superlatives, 20
supper, 71
synagogues, 124
talk, 156
tango, 50
taxi, 46
tea, 71
technology, 54
telephone, 47
temperature, 92
the moon, 86, 221
theatre, 43
theatres, 125
there is / there are, 26
third, 106
time, 105
time words, 52, 72
title of, 18
top of, 18

town, 91
towns, 119
train, 45
transport, 45
trouble, 85
type of, 66
underground, 45
understanding, 85
uneducated, 36
unemployed, 36
unemployment, 54
unique roles, 78
unique things, 14, 15
universe, 15, 169
university, 88
usual, 19
variety of, 66
villages, 119
waltz, 50
warmth, 85
weak, 36
weather, 51
weather, 85
web, 53
week, 52
weekend, 52
weight of, 18
wind, 51
work, 85, 90
world, 15
wrong, 19
years, 74
yogurt, 156
young, 36
zoo, 44

ABOUT THE AUTHOR

Seonaid Beckwith has been teaching English to students from all over the world for more than ten years. She has an MPhil in English and Applied Linguistics from the University of Cambridge and runs the popular grammar website www.perfect-english-grammar.com. She lives in London, UK, with her husband and children.

Made in the USA
San Bernardino, CA
28 August 2019